The Thrifty Author's Guide to Launching Your Book

Without Losing Your Mind

Gail Z. Martin

Copyright ©2010 by Gail Z. Martin
Library of Congress Control Number: 2009941992

The Thrifty Author's Guide to Launching Your Book
Without Losing Your Mind

For information, address Comfort Publishing, P.O. Box 6265, Concord, NC 28027. The views expressed in this book are not necessarily those of the publisher.

First printing

Book cover design by Kimberly Brouillete

ISBN: 9781935361060
Published by Comfort Publishing, LLC
www.comfortpublishing.com

Printed in the United States of America

Upcoming Titles in the "Thrifty Author's Guide" Series:

- *Front-Page PR on a Cut Rate Budget*
- *Social Media Marketing for Authors: Friend, Follow and Tweet Your Way to Success*
- *Storming the Blogsphere: Marketing Your Book on Blogs, Podcasts and Web Video*
- *Book Tours that Kick Butt*
- *Outrageous (Yet Professional) Book Promotions*
- *Book Web Sites That Wow Readers, Impress Reporters and Make Your Mother Proud*
- *From Published to Platform: How to Turn Your Book into a Speaking Career*

Table of Contents

Introduction

Every time I went into a bookstore before my first book, *The Summoner*, was published, I would find the spot on the shelf where my name would be alphabetically. After moving the other books aside, I would put my hand in that empty space and envision my book being there someday. When that day finally came, it was all I could do not to jump up and down screaming in the local bookstore. Little did I know it, but *the hard work had just begun.*

I was lucky to have a very supportive publisher, but even so, I could see that wouldn't be enough. After all, approximately 200,000 – 400,000 books are published each year just in the U.S. (figures vary depending on who's counting and what's included). Even within my genre niche, several hundred new books were going to debut within months of mine. I realized that the greatest book in the world can't sell if no one has heard about it. I also realized that publishers won't invite you to write a second book if your first one doesn't do well. I made it my business to make sure my books do well.

When my first book was published, I promised myself that, no matter how everything turned out, I was going to do everything possible to make my books successful. I've learned a lot as my series has progressed. I've seen some techniques work beyond my wildest imagination, while a few fizzled. Now, I want to share those insights with you so that your new book has the best chance for success. This book shares my secrets for successful book tours, attention-getting internet promotions, exciting websites and dynamic media interviews. You'll also discover tips I gathered some of my author friends, who have learned the hard way what worked and what didn't.

You don't have to be an extrovert to make these techniques work for you. Many of these techniques can be done online without ever having to go in front of a crowd. If you're not shy, there are more options open to you. Likewise, you don't need a degree in marketing to market your book successfully. On the other hand, anything you've ever learned or observed about successful sales and marketing won't hurt. So dive in with enthusiasm. Experiment, remix and recombine my suggestions. Find an approach that works for you. Just get out there and live your dream!

Chapter 1: *Marketing Is the Author's Responsibility*

Congratulations! You've finished writing your book, and you've either found an agent who found a publisher, or you've arranged for a publisher yourself. That means the hard part is over, right? Wrong! In fact, the hard work is just about to begin.

For people who like to write books, *writing* is the fun part. Authors love to tell a story or share knowledge. Even the research and editing is enjoyable, because writers understand how it fires their imaginations. When the final editing is complete and the manuscript goes to the printer, most writers heave a sigh of relief, then collapse into a chair. They assume that the publisher or the bookstore will sell their book while they go on to the next project. It doesn't work that way.

A Great 19th Century Business

Publishing is an industry where profit margins are surprisingly slim. That's because publishing hasn't changed much since the 1800s (which is a problem that is only gradually being addressed). It costs a lot of money to edit, format and design a book. Plus, it costs more money to print it, warehouse it, ship it, and take back unsold copies from bookstores. E-books eliminate most of these problems, but until they catch on with a majority of readers, authors must make do with the realities of traditional publishing. All those expenses leave very little extra cash for marketing.

Yes, it seems like books written by celebrities get the biggest ad budgets, and they do. That's because publishers, who have paid hundreds of thousands, and perhaps even millions of dollars in advance, have to make their money back. That leaves less—or no—money to promote new authors who need the marketing the most.

The Rules of Promotion Have Changed

The kinds of promotion publishing houses have traditionally paid for, such as shipping huge quantities of review copies to newspaper reviewers and placing big ads in major industry magazines, aren't working as well in today's Internet-driven world. Many major newspapers have disappeared. This has happened because fewer and fewer people read newspapers. Magazine readership has also dropped. Among those that have survived, many have stopped reviewing books. So the traditional, expensive, publisher-driven techniques aren't as valuable as they once were.

Thousands of citizen-journalists that are dedicated to every taste and genre have replaced the big newspaper book reviewers. Websites, book review sites, book-themed podcasts, book-focused Internet radio shows, book-related social media sites or groups and online discussion forums have sprung up to take the place of the traditional media. There are more of these new outlets than there were newspapers and magazines. Best of all, writers can access these new opportunities for free.

Free = Hard Work

Let me qualify *free*. I mean *free* as in not costing money, but not *free* as in not requiring effort. None of the techniques in this book require you to spend money or hire someone to help you; although you may find that you prefer to do so to speed things along. The truth is that, if you're willing to invest the same kind of elbow grease in marketing that it took to write your book, you can reach a global audience for the price of a high-speed Internet connection.

Mega-blockbusters, like the *Harry Potter* or *Twilight* series, and big names, like Stephen King or Clive Cussler, sell hundreds of thousands or even millions of copies. But the average book printed in the U.S. sells 7,000 copies or fewer. Many authors struggle to sell even that many copies. Now you see why promotion becomes essential for authors who want to continue publishing, and perhaps make some money.

A Quick Recap of Publishing Reality

When you sell a book to a publisher, some authors receive a promise of royalties, unless you wrote a book that is a work-for-hire project. If you received an *advance*, you must sell enough books for the publisher to recoup the cost of your advance before you receive royalties. The real meaning of *advance* is "an advance against royalties." It's like a draw on commission in a sales job. If you don't sell enough books to *earn out* your commission, then you don't get royalties. If this happens, your book effectively *lost* money for the publisher, who will be reluctant to buy another project from you again.

If you self-publish, you have invested the entire cost of creating your book, so you have even more money at stake. You need to recoup those costs in order to break even, and before you can consider any sales to be a profit. If you don't sell those books, you have a debt to pay and nothing but boxes filled with books to show for it. Furthermore, it's unlikely that you would put up the funds to create another book.

Your book faces a lot of competition, so marketing is essential. Even the best-designed, best-written book shares bookstore space with thousands of other titles, most of which are just as attractive. As a reader browses down the aisle and sees your book, you want him to think, "I've heard of him/her." Recognizing the name of your book, or the name of the author, makes it more likely that a reader will pick up your book and read the back cover. Marketing is all about creating *name recognition*.

Different Authors, Different Goals

Would it surprise you to know that not every author has a goal of becoming a New York Times' bestselling author? While few people would turn down the honor if it were offered to them, there are other reasons that authors write, even a few that don't involve money.

Here are the other reasons to write a book:

1) You want to further a cause or educate people about something important;
2) You want to raise money for a charity;
3) You want to enhance your professional expertise to land more clients;
4) You are a professional speaker who needs a "back of the room" product; or
5) You are passionate about your topic or story and want to share it.

There are also other ways besides money to define *success*. These can include:

1) Voicing a minority opinion or changing the way people think;
2) Recording something important for posterity;
3) Sharing information that saves or changes a life;
4) Providing insight or *how-to* knowledge on a subject with a small, but passionate audience; and/or
5) Providing a regional or special-interest view on a subject that is underrepresented.

Control Is a Good Thing

When you decide to lead the marketing effort for your book, you're taking control over the fate of your own creation. The publisher (if you have one) is risking his investment in designing, printing and distributing your book. You as the author are risking your future as a commercially viable writer. If you're a self-published author, then you also have an investment in the boxes of books stored in your garage.

Ideally, you can work together with your publisher on marketing. In my experience, publishers are happy to find an author who is committed to the effort that is required to help a book rise above the average. You may find that there are some things a publisher can do that would be more difficult for you to do for yourself. This can include running an ad that features several of the publisher's recent titles (including yours) in the trade journals read by bookstore buyers and publishing professionals. In addition, it can include negotiating with bookstores for better in-store placement, and creating posters or display materials. It might even include having a table at a big industry trade show or event like Book Expo of America (or one of the smaller, regional book shows) where you could do a signing or make an appearance.

Some publishers really don't have the budget to do more than print the book. In that case, see if you can gather valuable contacts and suggestions from them as you embark on your marketing mission. That can include introductions to other authors who may be interested in joint promotions or shared expenses, or referrals to influential bookstore owners or library buyers who can put in a good word for you. You won't know what's available to you until you ask, so don't be shy.

In this book, you'll learn how to plan for the three critical stages of your book's birth: pre-launch; launch; and post-launch. When you have a plan, you have a road map. This means you can create activities that move you closer to your goals, and you can avoid actions that waste time and money. You have control, and that's a good thing. No one in the world cares as much about your book as you do. That's why you need to control its destiny.

Gail's Tip

There's nothing better than connecting with readers who share your passion. Marketing enables them to find you and make that connection.

Assignment 1: Your Marketing Skills Inventory

This is where we look at what your natural abilities, and how they can help you market your book. We'll also figure out what kinds of things you'd really rather not do. This way, you will know what tasks you may want to outsource or just avoid (at least for now). You can add other skills to the list as well.

Look over the following list of skills. Which are you comfortable with? Which make you uncomfortable? Use a yellow highlighter for the skills you possess, and a green highlighter for the skills that aren't quite *you*.

Skills	Marketing Uses
Writing	Preparing press releases, media kits, blogs, articles and other PR materials
Public Speaking	Greeting the public at signings; Speaking at workshops and conferences; Doing radio interviews
Research	Building media lists; Uncovering contact information for reporters, bookstores, etc.
Internet Experience	Researching or setting up a basic website or blog; Using Internet tools or applications
Social Media	Connecting online on Facebook, Twitter, MySpace and book-related sites
Organization	Setting up signings and appearances; Maintaining your contact list; Scheduling promotions
Graphic Design	Creating bookplates, stationery, business cards, bookmarks, posters, and a logo
Phone Skills	Scheduling signings; Pitching stories to reporters; Giving radio and podcast interviews

Collaboration	Setting up joint signings or panels with other authors; Connecting with other authors for shared publicity or shared sales promotions
Photography	Taking digital pictures or web video of your own events; Using a webcam

"Been There, Done That" Author Tip

"For your book to succeed, you must think of your writing as a business. When companies do business with other businesses it's called B2B; with consumers, it's called B2C. Writers doing business with their readers. I call **B2R — Book to Reader.** The halcyon days of the publisher sending authors on a ten-city book tour are long gone. Now it's time to adapt the mantra, "if it's to be — it's up to me!" Shift your mindset into marketing gear to reach the widest possible audience. An easy way to make this shift is to think B2R! Where are your readers en masse? The solution is to find those readers by using low-cost, high-impact media tools – a compelling website, an e-zine, a blog -- and continuing the conversation on your topic via social networking."

Authors Lena Claxton and Alison Woo, *How to Say It Marketing with New Media – A Guide to Promoting Your Small Business Using Websites, E-zines, Blogs & Podcasts.* www.newmediamavens.com.

Chapter 2: *An Author Is a Book's Best Friend*

No one in the world cares as much about your book as you do, not even your mother. Your publisher, your agent and the bookstore manager have lots of books and authors to worry about. As much as they may like you and/or your book, their time is shared with other authors and professionals. Your book's future depends on you.

Before the Internet, most readers never gave much thought to actually meeting the author of their favorite books. Outside of occasional local book signings, library readings and a handful of literary festivals, authors were a solitary lot, toiling away alone in an office. Big name authors might get interviewed on TV, but not often. Readers who wanted to contact an author had to mail a letter to the publisher, then hope the publisher would forward it to the author.

Everything changed with the Internet. People can now connect with other people in a whole new way. Authors don't have to wait to be invited onto a talk show, or be limited by geography to meet only the readers within driving distance of a bookstore or library. However, the Internet has also raised expectations. Because the means exists to connect, there has become an increasing obligation to do so. Now, writers who aren't actively communicating with readers are noted for their absence. In marketing, absence is *never* a good thing.

It might be nice to think that your book will rocket to the top of the bestseller lists on its own strength. But the truth is, people will never read that wonderful book if they don't know it exists. And, the best resource to help them find it is you, the author.

Reaching the Two Key Audiences

Book marketing requires reaching out to two key audiences: the media and the reader.

The Internet has opened up new opportunities to accomplish this, and made it less expensive. To promote your book successfully, you need to understand how these two audiences differ, and why you'll have to approach each group a little differently.

The Media

Under *media* you can include both online and offline book reviewers, reporters for newspapers and magazines, bloggers, webmasters, librarians and bookstore owners. Media outlets also include TV and radio hosts, podcasters, Internet radio programs, and even Twitter users with large followings. These are the gatekeepers who decide which books get mentioned and which books don't. They make recommendations to readers and customers, and they can drive sales up in large quantities.

You can think of these individuals as *influencers*, because their opinions influence others on whether or not to try a book. Not only that, but some of these influencers determine whether your book will be available at all. If librarians or bookstore owners don't think your book will be in demand, they won't stock it.

Selling your book isn't the media's goal. Their goal is to inform and entertain their customers or audience. A reporter who doesn't inform and entertain loses a reader. When a radio host doesn't inform and entertain, the listener changes the channel. The same is true for online media such as podcasts and websites. Audiences have very short attention spans, and very little patience with anything that doesn't interest them. So reporters, reviewers, bloggers and radio/podcast hosts are always looking for something new and different that relates directly to their audiences' needs. You as an author have to shift your thinking from, "how can I sell my book?" to "how can I hook the audience's interest with some useful information and entertain at the same time?"

The best way to do this is to link your topic to something everyone's already talking about — current headlines. If you're the author of a financial book, and the headlines are about a recession, pitch yourself as an expert on sticking to a budget, getting out of debt, or saving money in unexpected ways. If you've written a fiction book about a messy divorce, watch for a big celebrity break-up to talk about pre-nups, betrayal and private investigators.

I write a fantasy adventure fiction book series about ghosts and magic. You might think that someone who writes this genre would have trouble finding current headlines. However, just as I was getting ready for my second book tour, *Newsweek* published a poll showing that 77% of Americans believe in the supernatural. That study became the hook for my media pitches, helping me to land interviews for radio, podcasts, blogs and newspapers all over the world.

How do you find the media? This is where you have a choice between elbow grease and cash. You can buy media lists from organizations, such as ParaPublishing, that are compiled especially for book promotion. These lists can save you a lot of time, but they may not be tailored to your genre or your special niche. You can also compile a list yourself — an approach which is time consuming but thorough. You can hire someone to compile the list for you (not necessarily expensive if you find an assistant through Elance.com or Craigslist.com). Or, you can hire a PR agency to promote you to the media list it has compiled.

Obviously, the least expensive option is to compile the list yourself. Getting hands-on experience in list building is a valuable exercise. I advise doing at least some of your own list building because you'll learn a lot about what's available, and how the sites differ. You'll also get an idea of how many of each type of media are out there. This includes the number of chain and independent bookstores near you, as well as library branches. You'll also need to adjust your pitch for the personality of each host, reporter or site and make changes depending on whether you're contacting an interviewer, a librarian or a book store manager.

The Reader

We live in a "do-it-yourself" society. We've been trained to bag our own groceries, pump our own gas, and even update our own records at the doctor's office. So it should be no surprise that consumers now get their own news. In the pre-Internet days, you had to wait for the daily paper, the monthly magazine, or the six o'clock news. Today, consumers go to the Internet to get the information they want, when they want it—24/7.

In fact, today's consumer goes around traditional media in an increasing number of ways. If you don't want to be bothered by ads during your favorite TV show, just TiVo it and skip the commercials, or wait for the season to come out on DVD and get it from Netflix. Can't stand radio commercials? Plug in your iPod. And, as for newspaper and magazine ads, an increasing number of readers get their information from online editions, bypassing the paper format entirely.

So, while the media remains an important part of spreading the word about your book, they aren't the only game in town anymore. That means that it's essential for you as an author to make it easy to find out about your book online. Here are some key ways to do that.

• Your own website—This should be a home for everything about you and your books.

• Search Engine Optimization (SEO)—Figure out the keywords that readers look for to find a book like yours. Which words would they type into Google if they don't know your name or the book title? For example, would it be *budget*, *quick dinners*, or even *vampires*? Use a tool like Google Keyword Tool (it's *free*) to see which keywords get the most hits. They are the words you want to use in your website copy, your press releases, and anything you post online. Those words will work the best for helping your information come up closer to the top of a reader's search.

• Social media sites—Facebook, MySpace, Twitter, Shelfari, GoodReads, AuthorNation, BookMarket.ning.com and many other sites create online communities where readers and authors can connect. Readers can ask questions to authors, comment on books, post their own reviews, and refer friends to books they like.

• Online PR sites—Some of these sites are free, and some require a fee. The benefit of posting your press releases on these online distribution sites is that it creates more links to your book website. Search engines, such as Google, like to see lots of inbound links.

• Web audio and video—Posting a short video to YouTube is free. A good YouTube video can reach millions of viewers who are actually interested in the content (not heading out for a sandwich, like they do during a TV commercial). With a webcam, it's easy to record yourself, upload the video to YouTube, then put a copy of the video onto your website. Programs like AudioAcrobat make it just as simple to record a greeting, or even a short reading from your book. Then you can put that link on your homepage, attach it to an email, or post it on your blog.

• Your own blog—A blog can be a great place to continue a conversation about your books. If you write nonfiction, you can blog on related topics and tie-ins to headline news (remember, your job is to inform and entertain!). Fiction writers can blog about everything from the process of writing to providing "how-to" information for would-be authors. Readers feel that they get to know you through your blog, and today's consumer wants a relationship, not a sales pitch.

Remember, your voice is your book's voice. You can be your book's best friend by connecting effectively with media and readers through free, online tools.

Gail's Tip

Informing or entertaining is a must. Informing *and* entertaining is a home-run!

Assignment 2: Topics for Media and Readers

• Brainstorm a list of topics that are related to your book. For example, if you've written a book about fitness, topics might include: weight-loss, looking good, health, staying young, reducing the risk of disease, etc.

• Next, create a table like the one below. Take each of the topics from your brainstorming list and decide whether they are best for media or readers. (Hint: You may need a slightly different angle for media than for readers.) Then, look for something in current news headlines to make your topic relevant and hot. Here's an example table for a hypothetical fitness book

• Add two new columns to your table: *Outlet* and *Message*. Under *Outlet*, write down the type of media best suited for your book. (A visual story is great for TV, but something that requires a little more explanation is usually better in a newspaper or blog.) In the *Message* column, make notes on how you might tweak the "hook" to suit the characteristics of that particular media.

Media Topics	Reader Topics	News Hook
Out of shape employees cost companies more in health expenses	Save money by getting fit	National obesity rates; Rising health insurance costs
Gyms see spike in work outs as pink slips increase	Tri down for better job prospects	Company layoffs; Unemployment statistics

"Been There, Done That" Author Tip

"One key point to think of when marketing is that you aren't marketing a book. You're marketing yourself. A single book may have a limited shelf life, appearing and disappearing in stores in the span of a year or two. Your marketing efforts, if you want to make a career, have to be geared around selling a body of work, not just a single book. So, whatever your marketing push is—blogging, going to cons, podcasting—it's important to think of it not as a six-month push for a single title, but as a decades long effort at making your name known and interesting to as many people as possible."

James Maxey, author of *Bitterwood. Dragonforge and Dragonseed*
http://dragonprophet.blogspot.com/

Chapter 3: *The WIIFM Principle: What's In It for Me?*

WIIFM stands for "what's in it for me?" In every book marketing project, there are three categories of people asking this question: the author, the readers and the media.

The Author

Every marketing action you take, every dollar you spend, and every hour you invest should tie back into one of the goals we talked about in the *Introduction*. If your marketing actions don't support your goals, then either your goals are wrong, or your marketing action is off-track.

It's easy to get so caught-up in all the opportunities to market your book that you stop evaluating whether each opportunity is going to help you achieve your goals. Clear goals will help you create a budget, prioritize your time, say "no" with less guilt and "yes" with confidence.

Remember, your ultimate goal is to let readers, who are interested in your particular kind of book, know that your book exists so they can buy it. You're not trying to reach every reader in the world, only the readers who read the kind of book you've written. In marketing language, the readers who read the kind of book you've written are your "target audience." To market your book effectively, you must either reach that target audience directly, or have your message relayed by people who do reach them directly (the media).

How well do you know your target audience? Here are some characteristics to consider:

- Age
- Gender;
- Education level;
- Income level;
- Hobbies and interests;
- Biggest concerns/worries;
- Personality type;

- Preferred location for buying books;
- Library usage;
- Internet habits; and
- Other media read or watched.

The more you know about your target audience, the better you will be able to put together marketing messages that appeal to them. No book is perfect for everyone. Without a clear idea of your target, you will waste time and energy promoting to those who don't buy your type of book, or focusing on media that doesn't cover your story because their audience isn't interested.

On the other hand, when you are clear about your target audience, you can uncover unexpected and authentic ways to reach out to them. You know where they go, what they do, and what their other interests include. For example, I understand my fantasy readers because I was a fan long before I became an author. I already knew that science fiction/fantasy readers love to go to genre conventions to meet authors and celebrities from favorite TV shows and movies. I also knew that fans were early and intense Internet users, and were quick to adopt podcasts and Internet radio. But what I also realized was that people who like to read fantasy adventure also like to attend Renaissance Festivals. Adding appearances at Renaissance Festivals was a successful way to broaden my reach to a highly receptive audience.

The Reader

A reader wants to be informed or entertained. If his or her main goal is entertainment, then learning something may or may not be considered a bonus. However, if the main goal is to be informed, an entertaining approach is definitely a plus.

Readers who want to be informed usually need to solve a problem. For example, they may need to fix a leaky faucet, improve their credit score, apply to college successfully, get in shape, or address a health or relationship concerns. An *information* reader is on a mission. He or she is likely to search by topic (Remember those keywords I talked about!), and will probably read more than one book on the subject.

No one wants to read a dry, boring book. That's why a light touch is important, even in an informative book. So, if you are marketing your book to information readers, remember that they are looking for content and readability. Create marketing messages assuring the reader that your book answers their questions and is easy to read. Give your reader tidbits of very useful knowledge in a brief, easy-to-remember and fun way. Apply the information directly to real-life situations so the reader can make a connection to his own problems. Use lots of examples and colorful abbreviations to make it easy to remember.

Entertainment readers can come in two styles: *pure entertainment* and *sneaky learners*. The pure entertainment reader looks for an escape from the real world. This person is likely to be reading fiction, specifically genre fiction. Sneaky learners enjoy learning for the sheer sake of knowing new information, as long as it's presented in an entertaining way. (Think about people who watch *The History Channel* or readers of *National Geographic*.) Sneaky learners may read history, biography or "how-to" materials because they like to learn. Or, they may read fiction to enjoy learning about exotic locations, historical events, or new technology. Science fiction readers, for example, expect good scientific information. They also enjoy learning something new, as do readers of historical romance, military fiction, and other genres.

To reach the sneaky learner, you'll need a message that promises entertainment with some tantalizing new tidbits of information. For example, readers of Dan Brown's *The Da Vinci Code,* enjoyed a thrilling suspense novel, but also learned a lot about church politics, ancient heresies, doctrinal arguments, and religious controversies. Authors Michael Crichton and Kathy Reichs incorporate cutting-edge technology and science into their thrillers, stoking the armchair expert's thirst for knowledge. At the same time, they provide pulse-pounding adventure.

The Media

You already know that the media wants to inform or entertain, and would prefer to do both. But more than that, the media wants to keep their readers or listeners so that the host, blogger, reporter or TV anchor keeps his or her job. Bored readers or listeners will always go somewhere else. Whenever too many listeners stop listening, or viewers change channels, ratings plummet and heads roll. A 24/7 media cycle means the need for news is never-ending. The truth is that the media is always looking for fresh stories, and they find those ideas from press releases.

Can you share a story that will make new readers pick up a copy or click on a story link? Is your interview interesting enough to make listeners or viewers stay tuned? Will enough people need your information or enjoy your topic to build web traffic?

For the media (both traditional and online), content is a means to drive more traffic to their newspaper, magazine, blog, podcast, radio show or TV program. It's also how book stores and libraries keep enough traffic in their facilities to stay open.

Your job as a guest is to drive traffic, whether you're being interviewed or doing a live event. So, while you are doing an interview or publicity event, it definitely pays to publicize that you'll be interviewed or appearing somewhere! The media expects that you, as an author/expert, will bring a following of readers who want to know more about your books or topic. Once they publicize you in order to retain and build traffic for themselves, you can tailor a message that meets the needs of their audience. You can also use their format to deliver a fun, informative and memorable appearance. When you deliver an audience to them, the media is more likely to invite you back. The more you appear, the bigger your audience grows, and the more in-demand you will become with the media who want to benefit from your following.

Assignment 3: Reaching Your Target Audience

• Write a profile for your ideal target reader. Include as many details as you can.

• Do your target readers require entertainment or sneaky learning? Where will you find them aside from bookstores? How can you tie your book into either entertainment or sneaky learning?

• What informative and entertaining messages can you offer to the media, based on your book?

"Been There, Done That" Author Tip

"It's critical to remember the essential answer to asking yourself, *"What is my most important job?"* Your most important job is to fuel being inspired.

"It's so easy to be caught up in the to-do lists, deadlines, email solicitations offering amazing results from the latest become-rich-and -famous strategy. Or, feel guilty about all the marketing things you should be doing, yet haven't achieved yet. Be true to your authentic mission, why you wrote your book, and find the joy in making a difference with your destined legacy. Remember the airlines telling you to put the oxygen mask on your face first, then sick grandma or baby. It all starts with you being well-fueled first. When you are aligned with your true inspiration, then you will be successful by serving the world with the gifts you were meant to contribute, and attract the right opportunities."

Marian Baker, author of *Wake Up Inspired—Fuel Healthier Success and Love the Life You're Meant to Lead.*   www.WakeUpInspired.com.

Chapter 4: *Reality Check—How Book Marketing Really Works*

Most of us *know* what we think we know by observing how the world around us seems to work. And for most new authors, what we *know* about book marketing comes from noticing what happens at bookstores and in the media for other authors.

So, this is how we *think* book marketing works. Major newspapers begin running author interviews or book reviews a few months before the books becomes available. Authors are on TV and radio, talking about their books and themselves. Bookstores hang huge posters to announce new books, put up signage, and move display units filled with new books to the front of the store.

We assume that the media is notified when an author will do a book signing. In our media-induced vision, fans line up an hour in advance for a good spot in line, clutching their copy of the book. The author is ushered to a prime location, where he or she begins autographing the books. Occasionally, he or she looks up to make witty conversation until the long line of fans is finally gone.

The problem with this scenario is that it is only true for the small percentage of authors who have reached the pinnacle of success. This includes authors whose prior books have established their reputation, and those who have built a following and are expected by the publisher and bookstores to sell hundreds of thousands (maybe even millions) of copies. It's also true if the author is already famous for something else—a TV or movie celebrity, a rock star, a recognized business leader or CEO, or even a news-worthy victim or hero. However, for the vast majority of authors, especially new ones, reality is a little different.

Months before your book comes out, you or your assistant compile a list of media and bookstores. Then, you begin to make phone calls, either pitching yourself as a guest or trying to book a signing. If your verbal pitch is intriguing, the reporter/host or the bookstore manager will ask you to send more information, including the ISBN number. This is a polite way to find out whether you are self-published. Unfortunately, unless you can verify that you have already sold thousands of copies of your self-published book via the Internet or other means, many traditional media outlets and big chain bookstores will not schedule you. Sometimes, you can get around that if you are a local author, or if your book has a local or extremely topical angle. However, the stigma in traditional channels is still highly against self-publishing.

If you are working with a publisher who has a book distributor under contract, your next hurdle is to make sure that the stores that agree to have you come for a signing will stock the book. If there is no book, then there won't be a signing. If you've self-published, this means planning to haul the books you'll need for the event in the trunk of your car. For authors who aren't J.K. Rowling, selling one to twenty books is considered very successful for a two-hour signing. There are a lot of factors involved, including the weather, the number of walk-in customers the store gets, and the amount of parking availability and traffic congestion. Your signing can be also be negatively affected if there is a major event competing for attention. It also matters where your signing table is located in the store.

National media covers a tiny fraction of the hundreds of thousands of books that are published in the U.S. each year. Your best bet is to focus on papers where you have a personal connection—hometown, current city of residence, cities where you'll be appearing at signings, your alma mater, etc. Take heart though. The Internet is bursting with blogs, special-interest websites, podcasts and Internet radio shows that cater to genre tastes. You still need to have a good pitch to show your potential to give a good interview, or to convince the reader that you have a good book for review. It's in your favor that there are hundreds of these sites, and they're not as heavily flooded with pitches as *The New York Times*, so your odds are dramatically better.

Do not, I repeat, do *not* regard these Internet media opportunities as second-rate. Treat them with the same respect and preparation you would give to *Good Morning America* or *The Washington Post*. "New" media is the wave of the future, and many of these sites have as many or more followers as some of the struggling "major" newspapers. Be polite, show up on time, speak in sound bites and always say 'thank you.'

Bookstores

Let's get back to reality. Most bookstores are overwhelmed and understaffed. Some will put up signage about your appearance, but others won't. Some have a newsletter where they promote upcoming authors, but they don't always think to add you if you don't ask. It's legitimate to ask how they can help you get the word out. After all, it brings traffic to their store. A few stores may even send out monthly press releases about events. Promotion varies widely depending on whether or not the store has a dedicated marketing person, and whether that person is excited about your book.

Be aware. Sometimes a store's manager or marketing person may have a personal bias for, or against, certain types of books (for example: non-fiction over fiction, literary books over genre novels). You probably won't know whether that's the case until you get to the store. You can also ask around and find out whether authors of equivalent fame are treated equally. If you think the bookstore staff have disdain for your genre or topic, cross that store off your list for future promotions. (But remember that store managers and marketers change frequently and their replacements could have a different mindset.) Live and learn. Next time, choose a venue that values your type of book.

Most bookstores make a good faith effort to help you succeed, but marketing may not be their strong point. Always call before you show up, just in case your books haven't arrived. It helps to have a small stash of your own that you can bring if necessary, and have the store reimburse you. Sometimes, scheduling mistakes are made, or the person who booked your event gets fired and forgets to tell anyone that you are coming. Calling a few days in advance of the signing can give you time to prepare for and to deal with problems. I'd also suggest that you offer to mail or email posters, along with a press release, and even card-sized *shelf-talkers* about your event to the store a few weeks in advance. (A *shelf-talker* is a card with a thumbnail-sized book cover and a short, attention-getting comment about your book. Independent booksellers love to put shelf-talkers beneath books to draw attention. You can make great looking shelf talkers using the backside of perforated postcard stationery from an office supply store.)

You'll also want to find out where they will put your signing table. If it's not right inside the front door, ask to be moved! It's also legitimate to ask for them to make short announcements over the PA system at the beginning and middle of your signing event so that people who are already in the store know you're up front.

Arrive early at the store and set up. If you've brought your own books, you'll need to carry those in, as well as whatever bookmarks or props you plan to use. You'll need to arrange your table and check in with the manager. Then, you wait for people to show up. It's important to realize that few of the people you encounter will have come because they knew you were there, even with excellent pre-event marketing. It's unlikely that you'll have a line.

Remember the front-of-store book placement and the cardboard display units? Believe it or not, those cost extra—sometimes tens-of-thousands of dollars extra. If your publisher doesn't pay for that kind of placement, the odds are against your getting it unless there is a section for local authors or it is an independent bookstore.

Posters and in-store signage will vary by store. Some stores are good about making their own. Some will put up posters if you send materials that look suitably professional. Other stores just aren't into it. Usually, if you bring your own posters and signs to use during the event, a store will display them. Make it easy for the staff. Be willing to do the placement, and take the signs down yourself. (If the store did make nice signs, you can ask to take them with you. There may be a way to salvage part of them for re-use.)

Even if no one shows up, BE POLITE to the store staff. Remember, they decide whether or not to stock your book. It's not their fault if it rains, or they have slow foot traffic. I have heard horror stories from bookstore staff about authors with attitude problems, and it's sad. If it's a slow day, make conversation with the staff. Most book store employees like to read, and they are often asked for recommendations by shoppers. Be interesting, likeable and polite, and your odds of being recommended will rise.

Media

If you have a media interview, it will probably be by phone. Find a quiet place with a landline telephone where you won't be interrupted by a barking dog or your children. Have a bottle of water just in case your throat gets dry. Avoid tapping your fingers, clicking a pen, or other nervous habits, such as swiveling in your chair. It can be heard, and creates background noise during a radio/podcast interview. Your mood needs to be *upbeat* so you can focus on providing entertaining value for the reader or listener. Answer their questions, and don't say "read my book." Be ready and waiting in position a few minutes before your scheduled time, and then stay there, even if the interviewer is late. Don't be defensive or have a chip on your shoulder. The media isn't out to get you. You are at much more risk of being ignored than railroaded. Most reporters are decent people trying to do their jobs, so make it easier on them.

There you have it. That's how book signings and media interviews *really* work for new authors. Don't be disappointed. Once upon a time, today's superstar authors were also new and unknown. As with any business, you have to pay your dues. It gets more comfortable with practice. In addition, as your reputation and following grows, bookstores and media will become more accommodating, even if you aren't at rock-star status.

Assignment 4: Preparing for Publicity Efforts

• Use the free templates, which are included with Microsoft® Word®, to make posters for your signings. Make sure to include your cover art and an attention-getting headline.

• Create shelf-talkers for bookstores by using perforated postcard stationery. Be sure to take them with you to signings, along with peel-and-stick tacky dots so you can stick the tags to the shelf.

• Think about how you will engage shoppers who come into the bookstore during your signing. Start with a smile and a friendly greeting. Don't forget to offer a bookmark and invitation to stop by and check out your featured book. Be ready with a short description that emphasizes user benefits, or that has an intriguing hook.

"Been There, Done That" Author Tip

J.C. Hutchins, author of *7ᵗʰ Son: Descent* and *Personal Effects: Dark Art,* created an audience for his writing through podcasting. The number of podcast listeners got the attention of a major publisher, and launched Hutchins' pro writing career. One of his latest ventures, *7ᵗʰ Son: Obsidian,* is an audio and video short-story anthology with thirty episodes that focus on his fictional world. Some of the authors are big-name professionals, while others are talented fans. What a great way to create loyal readers and stoke reader buzz! For more information, visit www.jchutchins.net.

"Whether you plan to self-publish or get a publisher, do yourself a favor and write a book proposal that includes a well-documented, marketing plan and publicity plan."

Ruth Klein, author of *The De-Stress Diva's Guide to Life*. www.RuthKlein.com.

Chapter 5: *A Word about Budgeting Money, Time and Resources*

Launching your book doesn't require a huge budget, but there are some expenses that are unavoidable. Here is a list of some basic expenses:
- Reserving a web domain;
- Creating a basic website;
- Printing business cards and/or bookmarks with your author information;
- Creating posters for your in-store events;
- Gas, food and lodging for speaking engagements and book signings;
- Phone calls; and
- High-speed Internet access.

In addition to out-of-pocket cash, launching your book will require a time commitment. It takes time to compile your contact lists, write your marketing materials and set up events. Either you will be doing this work (time), or you'll need to hire someone to do it for you (money).

Resources can also include other valuable elements that you may use to launch your book. This can include tapping personal favors from friends or colleagues, or converting a website or online profile from its current use to a book-related use. It may also mean converting "frequent flyer" miles or credit card rewards points to reduce your travel costs. Or, it could mean utilizing discount programs, coupons or other memberships to help achieve your launch goals.

Show Me the Money

Take a realistic look at your finances. How much money can you afford to spend on marketing? Remember that *marketing* includes printing business cards or bookmarks, making posters, maybe even hiring an intern or an assistant to help you with research. Don't be tempted to print your own business cards or bookmarks to save money. You will not look professional, and any savings will be at the expense of credibility. These need to be done right.

Shop around for a good deal on business cards, bookmarks and posters. Many authors are happy with Vistaprint.com or GotPrint.com. Don't rule out your office supply store or local printers, but be sure to investigate deals online. Make sure you understand delivery dates and shipping prices, and read the "fine print" to avoid surprises.

Once you know your budget, make sure you have some of the basics in place. If you don't already have a website, look at the cost of getting your name and your book title as a web address from a site such as GoDaddy.com. Creating a website doesn't have to be expensive. Template-driven sites, like Citymax.com, are inexpensive and easy to use, so you can create your own site and update it whenever necessary. Don't forget to account for travel and gas expenses to attend signings/events. Make sure that you also factor in the cost of a high-speed Internet connection if you don't already have one. You may even want to investigate cellular or home phone plans that enable you to make long-distance calls for free. This way you avoid a huge phone bill when calling reporters or doing phone interviews.

Where Does the Time Go?

Now, let's consider your calendar. Start with a book-style business calendar. I prefer a week-at-a-glance style, because it gives me room to write in hourly commitments for each day. Immediately mark out the times when you can't travel or be available for interviews, such as birthdays, holidays, family events, vacations, work obligations, etc. Remember that you'll be talking with people in different time zones. Keep in mind that evening for the East Coast will be afternoon for California, or early morning in other parts of the world.

Mark your "Launch Date." Look at the prime weekend dates that fall immediately after your launch. You will want to keep those free for signings. Look at the weeks just prior to your launch. You'll want to give yourself as much free time as possible for last-minute preparation. Reserve this time right now.

Figure out how many hours each week you can devote to marketing your book. You may want to block out an hour a day to make phone calls to media. You may want to reserve a portion of each day for emails, or as time to be available to schedule interviews. Plan ahead now to avoid scrambling later.

Your budget and your calendar will determine your geographic reach for live appearances. Can you stay overnight for an event? Can you be gone over a weekend? Factor in child care, as well as family/work responsibilities.

Resourceful Use of Your Resources

Resources come in many shapes and sizes. I listed a few types at the beginning of the chapter. Here they are again, along with some additional ideas:

- A web domain, using your name;
- Your existing blogs or social media sites that could be utilized;
- Professional memberships, especially those that include online profiles or possible opportunities to speak to groups;
- "Frequent flyer" miles or credit card reward points;
- Discount memberships—either warehouse clubs, such as Sam's Club or BJ's, or discounts you receive as a perk for membership in the Chamber of Commerce, AAA, AARP, professional clubs, alumni organizations or other groups;
- Rewards programs or volume discounts with Office Max, Office Depot, Staples and other national chains;
- Discounts on products or services through your bank or credit card;
- Discount websites, such as Travelocity or other reduced-fare programs;
- Friends in the business who would be willing to give you a discount or barter services;
- Access to college interns or industrious/reliable high school students, who might trade work hours for resume and portfolio experience;
- Contacts through your neighborhood, worship center, alma mater, as well as family and personal networks.

Most of us have access to more resources than we realize. How often have you renewed a club or organization membership and not even glanced at all the "free extras" that go with the membership? Some of the professional organizations I've belonged to have offered everything from shipping discounts to special offers from office supply stores and major computer brands. Credit cards often offer discounts on everything from rental cars to cell phone service. Start reading the flyers that come with your monthly bills. Also, check out the websites of the organizations you already belong to, in order to see how you can save money and leverage your dues!

Savings can come from surprising places. My grocery store's VIP customer card offers periodic rewards. I've earned wheeled luggage (handy for book tours), a gasoline gift certificate, and other perks that have helped to offset my travel expenses. Make sure that you sign up for the discount cards for Borders, Books-A-Million, Barnes & Noble and other stores to offset the cost of your research materials. If you'll be traveling, make sure to sign up for discount cards offered by fast food chains, national coffee shops, and quick-marts. Sign up for memberships with your favorite discount hotel chain to earn points toward free rooms or upgrades.

People are resources, too. Your cousin's teenage son might be willing to help you set up your Facebook page in exchange for an iTunes® gift card. Contacting a local university, technical school or community college might connect you with a student videographer who could create great web video at a fraction of the cost of hiring a professional. You may be able to work out barter arrangements for everything from printing to graphic design.

Don't forget the value of introductions and referrals. Ask your friends and colleagues to recommend organizations that might need a speaker, or to introduce you to their web designer and other professionals. If you're planning to travel, tap family and friends for a free night on the couch in cities where you'll be speaking or promoting your book.

Assignment 5: Finding Readers and Resources
- Make a list of all the discount clubs and professional memberships you already have.
- Visit their websites and look for the discounts.
- Check out online sources for services (such as Elance.com) and supplies (such as Ebay.com), as well as major office supply stores' websites. You may find "online only" coupons that enable you to save more.
- Ask everyone you know for referrals to the types of products and services you will need.
- Make sure to ask stores you frequent whether they offer any kind of discount, reward, or frequent-purchaser programs.
- For things you'll need frequently, such as photocopies, you may get

a deal by pre-purchasing in bulk. (For example, buy a reloadable gift card that offers you a discount per copy, if you buy 100 copies up front.)

'Been There, Done That' Author Tip

"Here's a tip that seems obvious, but took me a while to figure out. As you start publishing books and doing interviews, take the time to keep a list of the people who have interviewed you, as well as a list of the people who write you fan letters. You will build up your own database of publicity contacts, as well as a core list of people who like your books. Year after year, as you build this, these two lists will become very valuable resources."

Kevin J. Anderson, author of *The Edge of the World* www.wordfire.com

Chapter 6: *Creating the Marketing Plan for Your Book*

Believe it or not, before you create a marketing plan for your book, you need to have a business plan. Yes, you will need a business plan for your book.

Why? Because what you want out of your writing career will impact how you market yourself and your book. Remember what we talked about in Chapter One. We discussed how there were different reasons to write a book, and different definitions of success. In order to create a marketing plan that achieves your definition of success, you will need to think about why you're writing your book, and what you want out of your writing career.

Scenario 1: You've always wanted to be a writer. Your stories are alive for you, whether they are fiction or non-fiction. Writing puts you in the "zone" where you feel most alive. You want to share your stories with others. For you, writing and the story itself are the key goal.

Scenario 2: You write as a means to an end. You have subject matter expertise that is in demand, and you have back-end products or services you want to sell. For you, a book is a way to expand your professional credentials, to land bigger and more lucrative publishing and speaking contracts, and to attract more clients to buy more profitable products from you.

Scenario 3: You write about a cause to change the world. Your book could be inspirational, a "how-to" book, or even an expose. You are an advocate first and a writer second. Your book is a way to change hearts and minds and hopefully, policy or individual actions.

Scenario 4: You are passionate about a subject in which you've gained expertise, and you want to share that passion with others. Or, you may wish to gain credibility among others who already share your passion. Your book might be a family history or a biography, or perhaps it's a book about Shakespeare, origami, or re-enacting Revolutionary War battles. You already know it's not a book for the masses, but you want to be known and respected among your peers, and to contribute to the body of knowledge about your topic.

We have seen four different scenarios with four different goals, and four vastly different marketing plans. All books are not created equal. As you see with the scenarios above, the goal and the intended audience will make a big difference in the type of media you target, the pitch you create, and the coverage you can expect. Your goal and audience also impact your distribution decisions, ultimate income, and business objectives. In addition, they affect the kind of book promotion that is likely to be effective.

Basics of a Book Business Plan

A "book business plan" isn't the same as you'd use to get a loan for a company. It's a shorter version that is especially helpful to use as a springboard for an on-target marketing plan. Think about which of the above scenarios comes closest to your reason for writing your book. Next, on a blank sheet of paper, do your best to answer these questions.

- What is the *transformative value* of your book? How does it solve a problem for the reader, or provide value (entertainment, enlightenment, ideas, etc.)?
- Describe your primary target audience in detail (age, gender, education, location, income, key concerns, hobbies, aspirations, etc.).
- Justify why this is your primary audience.
- Now, identify your secondary audience and justify its position.
- Next, identify your tertiary audience and justify its position.
- Do a SWOT Analysis. Your SWOT analysis should make clear your Strengths, Weaknesses, Opportunities and Threats. Your business plan should have a goal or action that addresses each SWOT aspect.
- What are your book's STRENGTHS and features that differentiate it from other books on the same topic?
- What are the WEAKNESSES of you or your book? (Examples could range from lacking a distributor for your book, to having less career success in your topic than competing authors.)
- What OPPORTUNITIES currently exist in the marketplace for books such as yours? (For example, during an economic downturn, books on budgeting and saving money soar in popularity.)

- What are the biggest THREATS you see to the book's success? (This could range from you suddenly getting too busy with family, health or work issues to suitably promote the book, to having a crisis occur that makes your topic out of favor.)
- Do a "competitive analysis." What research or data gathering have you done to understand who your competition is? What threat do they pose? How do their services/audience/service areas overlap with yours, and how might you turn weak competitors into strong collaborative partners?
- Determine your annual marketing budget in dollars. How did you arrive at that figure?
- Determine your annual marketing budget in time. How did you arrive at that figure?

Once you have thought through these items, your book business plan should get clearer. If you are writing in order to promote other products or services, or to promote yourself as a speaker and/or consultant, then your goals will focus on reaching an audience of good prospects for your other products. If you are writing for the love of the story, you have a goal of selling enough books to make it commercially attractive for you to write more books (either to a publisher, or to yourself, if you are self-published). If it's the love of the topic that draws you, then you'll need a clear understanding of where there are gaps in available materials on that subject so that you can make an authoritative statement. And, if you want to change the world, you'll need to get a sense of how fresh and well-substantiated your approach is, so you can make a splash and fend off detractors.

The Book Marketing Plan
Once you have a clearer picture of your book business plan, come up with your top three business goals and put them in priority order. For example, a writer who wants to establish a sales platform may have these goals: 1) Attract media attention as an expert; 2) Establish topic/industry credibility; and 3) Fill rooms with qualified prospects who can buy products/services or back-of-the-room books. In contrast, a writer who wants to change the world might have these goals: 1) Attract media attention to a specific need/cause; 2) Create a way to organize or raise

funds; and 3) Mobilize readers to take action.

A writer with a subject passion might choose these goals: 1) Attract attention within the narrow niche of media focused on that particular subject; 2) Get invitations to speak at seminars, conferences and other programs pertaining to that subject; 3) Win an award, have an article or excerpt in a prestigious industry publication, or achieve some other kind of in-group recognition as a "subject master." And, a writer with a story could have these goals: 1) Attract media attention for signings or for the launch of the book; 2) Connect with readers who share a passion for that kind of story to sell books, as well as establish relationships; and 3) Remain connected to readers as the springboard to sell other books in the series.

Once you have your business plan goals, link each goal to a specific target audience. Some examples of target audiences include: readers, hobbyists, and professionals within an industry or specialty; academics; the professional media; new media (blogs, podcasts, etc); bookstore buyers; librarians; and conference event planners, etc.

Once you have determined a target audience for each business plan goal, it's time to match your marketing goals to the business goal/target audience. Make it easy on yourself. You shouldn't have more than five business goals (I would suggest starting with three), and don't try to create more than two marketing goals for each business goal. Avoid the temptation to think that every goal affects every audience. As you'll see when you try to match marketing to goals, the simpler it is, the better it will be.

Here's an example table for the sales platform writer:

Business Goal	Target Audience	Marketing Goal
Attract attention as an expert	Traditional and new media	Get name recognition linked to a subject
Establish credibility	Media, prospects	Become the go-to person for subject answers

| Fill rooms with prospects | Event planners, prospects | Get booked to speak and attract an audience |

Once you have your top-level marketing goals, now think about the specific actions you will need to achieve them. For example, considering the first goal of using the media to build name recognition as a subject expert, some specific actions might include:

- Build a list targeting all media that covers your subject;
- Create a pitch letter to obtain interviews or request reviews;
- Create a website that conveys a professional image;
- Create press releases to announce achievements and events; and
- Create basic marketing materials (business cards,bookmarks, posters, etc.).

The great thing about this method is that each marketing action is tied to marketing and business goals, as well as a specific target audience. This makes it easier for you to say 'no' to opportunities that aren't really right for you (and a way to know that they aren't right). It also gives you a guilt-free reason to say 'yes' to the opportunities that are a good fit. Now that you've created your marketing plan, let's match your to-do list with the actions it will take to make your marketing happen!

Assignment 6: Starting Your Book's Marketing Plan
- Use the tools in this chapter to create a preliminary marketing plan for your book. Have a couple of trusted friends read it over and give you feedback, then revise.
- Make sure your marketing plan aligns with your business plan, and include a budget to keep you on track.

"Been There, Done That" Author Tip
"Keep in mind that the best thing you can do to further your career is keep writing. Of course, you want to promote your book, but you can't reach every reader in the country and you shouldn't even make the attempt. Most books sell via word of mouth, either from store clerks or friend to

friend. A good book gets people talking and that sells books. And a good follow-up starts to build a reputation, which in turn starts to build a career. So write, and write some more, and keep on writing. That's what writers do."

David B. Coe, author of *The Sorcerers' Plague* and *The Horsemen's Gambit*. www.DavidBCoe.com

Chapter 7: *Six Months Until Launch*

Your book is written and you have a firm publication date. Now what do you need to do?

Don't underestimate the time and effort required to gear up for marketing, especially for your first book. You have a lot of work to do. If it's your first time, there is groundwork you'll be laying that you can build on for future book launches. This will save you a lot of time down the road. For now, however, you've got some set-up to do.

Your "Six Month Until Launch" Action List

Here are the key things to accomplish six months before your book launch.

- Compile a media list and a list of potential reviewers.
- Determine your time availability and set up a master calendar.
- Based on your time and travel budget, determine the geographic area in which you can make live appearances.
- Research the bookstores and events within that geographic area that are appropriate to your topic and business goals.
- Compile a list of bookstore managers and event coordinators.
- Set up a website and/or blog.
- Set up a Facebook page and a Twitter profile.

Investigate other social media sites where your target audience of readers is already congregating.

Let's talk about each of these items. It's important to start these items so early because they take time to put together. You also want to start them as soon as possible so that you will have them ready a few months before launch date. That's when you'll really need to use them or have them up and running.

Media List

The Internet has made media list research easier and more affordable than ever before, but it is still very time-consuming. Think about the types of traditional media your target audience utilizes. You may need to do some research if you aren't sure.

Remember that traditional newspapers have seen an audience decline for years, and now tend to reach a predominantly older reader. TV is heavily segmented, thanks to cable and satellite programming. Radio is also less dominant today, due to MP3 players and satellite radio.

Make sure you include specialty magazines, websites or blogs that cover your topic. Also, include podcasts or Internet radio programs for your topic, and local publications in areas where you expect to speak or do signings. Here's what you need to compile for your media list:

- Publication name;
- Call letters (for TV/Radio);
- Website;
- Host, reporter, editor, and reviewer names, plus email and direct phone numbers; and
- Notes about target audience, distribution, frequency of publication or show times, and any particulars about how to contact them for interviews.

Read or listen to a sample program for each media possibility. What's the style? What types of guests do they favor? Are they generally positive, or do they go for laughs at the expense of the guest? Avoid the "shock jocks" and the high-controversy shows, because they are likely to be an unpleasant experience. A word to the wise: Don't shoot for being on *Oprah*. Start small with low-risk interviews and reviews to practice and find out what works best for you. As you become better known and more successful, bigger opportunities will come your way.

Compiling your bookstore and event list works the same way. Create a separate spreadsheet. Note the location, plus the names of each bookstore, their manager and their marketing person. Make sure you also find out the best phone number to reach the person who books events. Don't forget to get an email address. You will usually need to call and speak to someone to get this, but it comes in handy. Make notes as you visit store/event websites or talk to managers or organizers on what they want or don't want, then do accordingly. You'll be able to get the phone numbers and addresses from the web, but you'll have to call and ask to get the name of the marketing manager or store manager.

Websites and Social Media

Avoid the temptation to use a free website that goes with your email address. These sites usually have long, incomprehensible addresses full of numbers and symbols. Your website address should be your name and/or your book title. If possible, reserve both. You can always forward visitors who type in one address to the actual location of the website. The key is to have a web address that is professional and easy to remember. If you can't afford to hire someone to build your site, use a template program, like Citymax.com (there are other similar programs available as well). Remember, your site is another way you will build credibility.

Social media like Facebook, Twitter and MySpace are free to set up. You'll want to be in places where readers can find you. Before you throw together a social media site, think of how you want to use it. What information do you want to share? Will you be sharing audio and video, as well as comments or text? Facebook now offers "fan pages" for authors, bands and others. These pages offer advantages over using a personal page to promote your book. It's the preferred way to create a presence on Facebook.

Investigate sites that are just for readers, such as GoodReads.com, AuthorNation.com, Shelfari, Armchair Interviews and similar sites. You can probably also find sites just for your specific genre or topic. Do research to find the best two or three sites before you dive in so that you're investing your time wisely.

Two sites that are important for you are Wikipedia™ and Amazon's® author profile page. Wikipedia is the user-created compendium of knowledge that allows readers to create, edit and update pages in the belief that the collective contribution will eventually get it right. Wikipedia takes a dim view of people putting up a page about themselves, but you can ask someone else to do it for you, whether that's a friend or an assistant. Take a look at pages for other authors and then write something similar, being careful to avoid promotion and puffery.

If your book is available through Amazon, then you can create an Amazon author profile. Not only is the profile available for readers to view to learn more about you, but your page also gives you a blog that automatically sends your update to everyone who has bought your book through Amazon. Amazon's page layout changes, but look for a navigation link for authors and follow the instructions.

Blogging is also easy to set up, and often free. You may get a blog as part of your website package, or you can set one up for yourself at sites, like Wordpress.com or LiveJournal. Be sure you read the rules to see if you are allowed to have a "commercial" blog on that particular platform, before setting up your blog.

Gail's Tip

Don't be afraid to share the blogging stage with other worth-while professionals. Invite some other professionals in related, non-competing fields to be a guest blogger on your blog. Also, let them know you are available to be a guest blogger for them. This provides helpful, fresh information to the blog readers, while introducing both you, and your guest, to each other's readers. You can also do this with newsletters.

Assignment 7: "Six Months to Launch" Checklist

• Start compiling your media list. Use Radio-Locator.com to help you find broadcast radio stations. Use PodcastAlley.com, PodcastPickle.com and BlogTalkRadio.com to find podcasts and Internet radio shows.

• To find newspapers, Google "newspapers in (city name)," and follow the links.

• Compile your information in a spreadsheet, like Microsoft® Excel, so it's easy to search and update.

"Been There, Done That" Author Tip

"Blogging is overrated and getting older by the second, but there is still no better way to reach your *existing* readers and your *growing* readership than to blog on your own blog site. Your daily life is boring? Include bits of prose you have to delete from a longer piece of work, excerpts, and funny photos of your kids. You can link to YouTube and put up amusing videos of your pet or your baby/grandbaby/niece/nephew/whatever. You need to start coming up with potential blogs about six months before your book comes out. Get into the habit and rhythm of blogging early, archiving the blogs so you will have ideas to draw on. These can be altered for each type of blog site you appear on. Remember—humor is good. If you can be funny, even about a subject that is difficult, it goes a long way to attracting readers to your book. Is your book too serious for humor? Even dark humor or a wry sense of the macabre is good for PR."

Faith Hunter, author of *Blood Ring*, *Seraphs* and *Host*. Faith also writes as Gwen Hunter (*Rapid Descent*) www.faithhunter.net and www.gwenhunter.com

Chapter 8: *Five Months Until Launch*

Last month, you started to get the essentials in place. Next you're going to build on that platform. It's important to accomplish each month's goals to avoid delaying future steps.

This month, you have a new set of challenges:

• Writing your pitch for bookstores and events;

• Researching options for printing bookmarks, posters, business cards, etc. (Don't forget to factor these into your budget.);

• Finding out from your publisher (or directly from your artist, if you are self-published) what limitations you have in using your book cover art for promotional purposes; and

• Compiling your speaker/author bio.

Basic Materials

You will need to check with your publisher (or the artist directly, if you are self-published) about your right to use the cover art for promotional purposes. This includes its usage on your website, business cards, posters and bookmarks, and any other medium in order to promote your book. Note: It is one thing to use cover art to promote your book. However, it's another to create t-shirts, coffee mugs, or other imprinted items for sale. If you plan to create and sell spin-off products using the cover artwork, make sure that permission from the artist is written into your contract with the artist upfront.

You will certainly need at least 500 business cards. Try to get a paper sample if you can. You will need to use a fairly stiff card stock so that it doesn't feel flimsy and cheap. The business card for your book should have the title and book cover graphic, your name as the author, your website address, an email address (preferably one that uses your book website with a dot com, such as Jane@mynewbook.com), as well as a phone number if you wish to make it available. Consider having the graphic for your book cover on the front of your card, with your contact information on the back.

You will also want to include your ISBN number, as well as your Twitter name and MySpace page so people can find you easily. The card should be in full-color, if at all possible.

I've had good success using a high quality business card as a bookmark, thereby making one piece do double-duty. However, I do see a lot of authors using bookmarks, and you may want a stash (at least 500 – 1,000) for your launch. One of the best ways to find good resources is to attend signings and writing conferences to ask other authors where they get their materials. A quantity of 500 – 1,000 is enough to give you a good printing price without incurring a big cost or creating a storage problem. It usually doesn't cost much extra money to increase card quantities, so always get estimates for more if you want to compare prices.

I'm personally not a big fan of postcards and other imprinted items. Postcards might be worthwhile if you intend to mail them to bookstores and reviewers, but you can create a digital version for less money and save yourself postage. Imprinted items such as pens, clips, etc. are very expensive. Unless the piece is very clever and has a direct tie-in to your book, these items tend to get lost in the desk drawer with all the other freebies from real estate agents and insurance salesmen.

Creating Your Bio

Now is a good time to start thinking about your author bio. Make sure that it is no more than one page long, and write using active verbs and short, snappy sentences. Pick details that highlight your credibility, but don't list every award you've ever won. Incorporate something fun and interesting, with a few details about hobbies or family. Make it personal and inviting.

Avoid the trap of mistaking your bio for a resume. Your bio should be in paragraphs, not in resume format. You don't need to list every job had, every major work or life accomplishment. Pare down your bio information so that you use the most significant and relevant information.

Your primary goal is to make it evident very quickly why *you* are a credible expert. Your bio also showcases accomplishments that directly relate to your book's topic. Make it readable and exciting. Consider adding a current professional headshot along with your logo, contact information and university degrees.

Listing your top professional memberships is nice also. If you have been interviewed on major media resources (CNN, MSNBC, etc.), then list the top two or three shows or channels. This will let potential media hosts know that you are a seasoned interviewee. If you haven't had that type of media exposure yet, don't worry about it. Just omit any mention of media. You can always add it later.

Your bio needs to be on your author website. You'll also want to include your bio in your press kit. (We'll talk about that later.) Once you have your full, one-page bio written, you can work on having several shorter versions. You need to write some with 500 words, 250 words and 100 words each. You'd be surprised how many times you'll be asked for a bio before an interview or speaking engagement.

This is a good time to get professional photos taken so you have a good head shot for your website and bio. If you're really strapped for cash, you can go to Wal-Mart or JCPenney's photography studios. Make sure to get the photos on disk so you can use the digital version. Be warned that these photos won't be the resolution you'll need for some professional applications, so they are truly a temporary fix. Ask around through your membership organizations for a referral to a local photographer who specializes in professional photos (these are called *headshots* and are not the same thing as portraits). You will probably want to have a couple of different shots taken so you have some variety (for example, a head and shoulders shot, a standing, three-quarters length shot, etc.). You may even want to bring a couple of different outfits.

Focus on credibility, approachability and professionalism, not glamour. Your hair, make-up, clothing and jewelry should be professional, not sexy. That means wearing a jacket, for both men and women. If your topic is very conservative (such as managing money), men should consider a coat and tie, and women should wear a jacket with a simple blouse and classic jewelry, such as pearls. For a more relaxed topic, a sport coat and shirt that opens at the neck may be appropriate for men, while women can go with more color or more creative jewelry.

Your Pitch Letter for Bookstores and Events

This is a good time to write a pitch to bookstores and event coordinators. Your goal is to schedule book signings at stores, as well as to get speaker invitations to events that reach your target audience. For bookstores, you'll be delivering your pitch via live phone calls. For event planners, you'll probably send it via emails.

Your pitch to bookstores should include your name, the book title and release date, your publisher, and ISBN number. (If you are self-published, list your ISBN number and whatever "imprint" name you have selected. You don't need to announce that you are self-published.) The pitch should also include the dates you'll be in the related geographic areas. Depending on your book topic, include that you are willing to offer to hold free workshops or 20-minute seminars, if appropriate. This can be a great hook for authors of "how-to" books, and can give stores an extra reason to promote you and your book.

Don't forget to ask the bookstore manager or marketing contact person for an email address, so you can confirm all dates and times in writing. You should include the short version of your bio with any emails. Ask if they can receive attachments then avoid attaching too many items (book cover art, poster graphics, etc.). This would make your emails very large, so it's better to break the information into multiple emails. If the recipient can't receive attachments, embed the information in the body of the email, or use a download site like Box.net or 4share.com in order to send a link to larger files.

For event planners, conferences and genre conventions, make sure you would be available for the event before pitching yourself as a guest. Write a friendly email that shows you have done your homework. Promote a topic that is of interest to the planner's audience, as well as suitable for the event. The majority of writing conferences and conventions do not pay a stipend, or reimburse for hotel or travel expenses until you are at the "guest of honor" level. However, the exposure can be priceless.

Whenever you send an email, remember to suggest several topics and include a short version of your bio. You must include your contact information and a link to your website. Remember that events often announce featured speakers six months or more in advance, so pitch conferences and conventions that are at least six months to a year in the future.

Plan to follow up on your pitch email with a friendly phone call. This is your chance to *sell* yourself to the event planner, but do so with a light touch. Make sure he or she received your email. Don't forget to give a brief recap of the reasons your credentials, as an author/expert, would make you a good fit as a panelist or speaker. If you've been a presenter at similar programs, you should mention a couple, but keep the list short. You probably won't get a *yes* or *no* on the spot, but you can ask for the planner to keep you in mind, Make sure to also find out when final decisions will be made. Always be polite and say 'thank you.' If you aren't chosen for this year, then inquire about next year. You are trying for long-term results, so don't be discouraged.

Gail's Tip

If you already have some experience with speaking engagements, see if you can get testimonials from event planners for those events. Including a few of these with your speaking pitch can make new event planners feel better about booking you if you aren't a *known quantity*. Make sure that you include the planner's name and the event with each testimonial.

Assignment 8: Bios and Pitch Letters

• Write a first draft of your bio. Give it to three trusted friends, who have an eye for professionalism, to give you an honest review. Next, tweak it accordingly.

• Get your photo taken.

• Draft your pitch letter for event planners and bookstores. Practice giving it to the mirror until you can do it conversationally. Avoid sounding like you've memorized a script. If you can, call up a friend to practice. Or, call your own answering machine and pitch yourself!

• Create an author business card. Printers and office supply stores can help with the design. Remember, people will judge the quality of your book by the quality of your card. So, make it professional!

"Been There, Done That" Author Tip:

"As an author, your work isn't done the moment you sign the contract. No matter if you are with a large publishing house or a small press, it is very important to start promoting your book well before the actual release date. The moment you have a deal, start talking the book up, and don't ever stop...if you don't show enthusiasm and interest in your book, then you very well can't expect your target audience to!

The Internet is an amazing tool for self-promotion, between blogs, podcasts, networking sites, and the endless databases out there, be sure to use every opportunity to make your name known. Create a mailing list people can sign up for, seek out author interviews or book reviews with the various sites that post such things. If it's free, moral, and legal, use it because in the world of publishing, you need every angle you can get!

Don't just try to sell people on your work; it is more important to make a connection with people than it is to make a buck by selling them a book. As an author, meeting up close and personal with those who can appreciate what I write is a blast and I find I've more than made fans, I've made friends. If you focus too much on the business side of what you are doing or making sure people are aware of what you have accomplished, it is not only one of the biggest turn-offs, it is also a quick way to take the joy out of being published.

You can't just sit back and wait for the royalty checks to come in if you want to make a (good) name for yourself in publishing. The one thing I always tell anyone asking for advice in this industry: You have to be as creative in your marketing as you are in your writing. Look for the angle. Look for what will stick out in people's minds. There are millions of books out there. What clever approach can you come up with to make them remember yours?"

Danielle Ackley-McPhail, author of the Eternal Cycle novel series and senior editor of the award-winning Bad-Ass Faeries anthology series. www.sidhenadaire.com.

Chapter 9: *Four Months Until Launch*

This month, you have a new list of ways to get prepared for your book launch. We'll be looking at:
- Writing your media pitch, reviewer letter and press kit; and
- Setting up speaking engagements or book signings.

Your Media Pitch, Reviewer Letter and Press Kit

Your media pitch is what you offer to radio or podcast hosts, TV shows and reporters/interviewers in order to persuade them to book you as a guest. Always include your reviewer letter with a copy of your book whenever you mail to online and offline book reviewers. Make sure that you feature important publication information, as well as enticing reasons to feature your book. The press kit is a helpful collection of information that reporters, hosts, reviewers, and even bookstore managers, can use to get correct information about you and your book.

Media Pitch

Your media pitch will have ten seconds or less to grab the attention of a busy reporter or radio/podcast host. Make it snappy and interesting, and focus on what you can do for their readers/listeners. Start with a catchy headline, but make sure (since you'll be emailing this) that it doesn't look like a "spam" message. Try to tie-in your topic to current headlines, if there is a real connection and it would not be in poor taste. In just a few sentences, explain how your can provide tips to solve a common problem or get a better outcome for their readers/listeners. You can even anticipate a few key questions that are tantalizing, and write a bullet point for each. Always include a very short (one paragraph) bio, plus contact information.

Hosts and reporters are busy people, and they get a lot of pitches. Media expert Wayne Kelly says that it takes at least seven calls or emails to get through to your average radio host. Most people give up after one, so the odds are in favor of people who are politely persistent. If you really want to study this subject deeper, I suggest Wayne Kelly's excellent site at OnAirPublicity.com™, or Jeff Crilley's book, called *Free Publicity*.

Gail's Tip

I begin my email subject lines for media pitches with a phrase to let the reporter know this is business. Examples of some titles I may use are *Guest Request, Press Release*, and *Media Alert*. I follow that phrase with a colon, and then go into the headline. This tends to give me a better chance against spam filters, as well as reporters with a "quick-trigger" deleting finger.

Reviewer Letter

Your reviewer letter should be personalized to the specific reviewer and publication/site. Include your publication information (book title, ISBN number, publisher name, release date and distribution), plus give a 75-word recap of the book. Make it clear (I usually use boldface type) that you are submitting the book for review. You can also include a short (fewer than 100 words) bio, plus details of any upcoming book tour or media events. Be sure to end the letter with a nice "thank you," and always offer to supply cover art or other information. Your contact information should be easy to find so that a reviewer who has questions can reach you.

On your first book, don't be surprised if you don't hear back from reviewers. You can follow up with a polite phone call or email to make sure the book arrives. Some people will be excited about it, others will be noncommittal, and some may even be rude. Cross the rude ones off your list for next time and just go on. Be extremely polite, and thank reviewers for their consideration.

Many reviewers will not email you when a review posts. So, it's a good idea to set up free Google Alerts (GoogleAlerts.com) to notify you whenever your name, book title, and/or company are mentioned anywhere online.

You can't guarantee that a reviewer will love your book, or write a positive review. Even reviewers who like a book may feel compelled to point out weaknesses, in order to appear balanced. When you get a positive review, write a nice *thank you* note.

When you get a negative review, take a walk around the block, and call your best friend to vent. DO NOT contact the reviewer. Make a note of anyone who is unduly negative or harsh, and don't send future books for their review. Sometimes, you can avoid heartache by reading other book reviews written by a reviewer prior to sending your book for consideration. If the reviewer hates everything or takes a snarky tone, it's probably better to drop that person from your list.

Your Press Kit

Your press kit should include several items:
- Your author/speaker bio, in varying lengths;
- Book summary, in varying lengths;
- A Frequently-Asked-Questions (FAQ) page;
- A concise interview with you as an author; and
- A short book review.

We've already covered how to write your bio, so let's talk about the book summaries. The easier you make it for a reporter or host to get your information right, the happier you'll be with the ultimate results. Make it easy for the media to describe your book by writing summaries for it in various lengths. I include a page with a one-sentence summary, as well as 50-word, 75-word, 100-word and 200-word descriptions. Not only do the media use these, but it makes it very easy for you to grab a quick description when necessary for program books, enhanced bios or other uses.

A Frequently-Asked-Questions (FAQ) page is your chance to raise all the questions that you wish an interviewer would ask. These can be questions about your expertise, the book subject, or how you came to write about the topic. They can focus on reasons people need the information (for non-fiction), as well as the research and background involved (for both fiction and non-fiction). You can also suggest story ideas by asking questions that have intriguing answers. This may also lead the media to promote future books by mentioning upcoming new titles, if those details are firm.

Writing an interview with yourself may sound odd, but I've had reporters in small town newspapers pick up the interview I wrote and run it word for word. It doesn't get any better than that! This is your opportunity to ask yourself the questions you want to answer, as well as highlight key information about yourself and your book. Keep the interview to one page, or about 500 words.

Providing a book review of your own can also be a great resource for a time-pressed reporter or interviewer. Of course, you'll focus on how the book is different and original, and use positive (but not hyped-up) terms such as *exciting*, *adventurous* or *easy-to-read*, depending on your subject matter. Don't overdo it (after all, it is your book), but on the other hand, don't feel the need to point out any weaknesses. Write the review you'd like to see in print, and keep it to about 500 words.

What Do I Do with a Press Kit?

Your press kit should be posted on your website. Make sure that it is located in a place that's easy for media and reviewers to find. You can include a link to this page in the signature block of your email. You should also mention that an online press kit is available (including the link) in your press releases, media pitches, speaking requests and review letters.

Send a copy of your press kit to your publisher. Remember, your publisher may use the information in their promotion efforts for your book, as well as include the link on their website. If you are meeting with a reporter or event planner in person, print out a copy of your press kit on nice paper. Be sure to slip it into a professional-looking pocket folder. I have personalized pocket folders by using full-page, self-stick labels. I printed out a color label of my book cover and affixed it to the front of a good quality, glossy pocket folder (card stock, not plastic) for a custom look at a do-it-yourself price. If your budget allows, you can send your press kit in a pocket folder, along with review copies of your book, to your top potential reviewers.

Assignment 9: Preparing Your Press Kit

• Write your press kit pages then show them to someone who hasn't read your manuscript. Quiz that person about what they understood just from reading your press kit. Revise accordingly.

• Upload your press kit to your website, and include the link in your pitch materials.

• Begin to pitch event coordinators using your press kit.

• Customize your media pitches to individual reporters, as well as your reviewer letter to specific reviewers.

"Been There, Done That" Author Tip

"Please don't overlook the easiest opportunity to promote your book... LOCAL media. The day you release your book, you should be making the circuit...Morning Radio Show, noon hour local cable show, newspaper interviews, and end it off with a book signing at your favorite bookstore. Even the smallest towns have media that is looking for local stories. The mandate of smaller market stations is to promote local people. You would be shocked at the number of local books that I would have loved to feature on my radio show...but never knew anything about them...until it was too late to help promote them."

Wayne Kelly, Radio Host/ Media PR Coach www.onairpublicity.com

Chapter 10: *Three Months Until Launch*

In this chapter, we'll start to see your previous preparation begin to pay off as you get ready for the big launch. Specifically, you'll focus on:
- Creating valuable content for your website;
- Blogging regularly about your topic;
- Using social media to stir up excitement; and
- Sending out your review copies.

Content, Content, Content

Today, knowledge is the most valuable resource. As an author, that is especially true. When you write, you convert knowledge into content. Your challenge is to go beyond providing the content of your book. You need to see how many ways you can repurpose, revise and reuse your knowledge, to provide content in as many venues as possible. That way you will expose people to your expertise, as well as promote your book.

Your website, blog and social media sites are places where you control all of the content. They are great places to establish yourself as a subject expert and thought leader, not just someone trying to hawk a book. It may be your goal to use your book as a stepping stone in order to snare more clients, or to attract paid speaking engagements. However, it will be your website, blog and social media sites that extend your professional voice, beyond the pages of your book, to establish relationships with prospects and event planners. Reporters, TV/radio/podcast hosts and reviewers will also visit your website, blog and social media sites to learn more about you. Welcome to life in a fishbowl.

Your website is a great place to show the full range of what you offer. If you have other information products (such as teleseminars, home study kits, etc.) in addition to your book, your website can introduce visitors to your range of products. If you offer professional consulting or coaching services, you can explain what you provide.

Your website is also a great place to give readers a "sneak peek" at your book. Offer a free chapter so readers can get hooked on the story or your great information. Include an interview with yourself, a Q&A section, even web audio and video. Using an inexpensive digital video recorder (usually under $200), you can make your own videos, upload them to YouTube, and add them to your website so that readers can put a face to your name. With a program like AudioAcrobat.com, you can use your phone to record an audio greeting or even to record yourself reading from your own book. You can then add that to your newsletter, blog or website. Don't be afraid to share tidbits of information. You're whetting the reader's appetite, and if the book is interesting, they'll want more!

On your blog, you can talk about the topics you cover in your book, whether the book is fiction or non-fiction. A blog is a great place to note how your book ties into current or recent headline news, seasonal trends or the business cycle. For example, my fiction series, *The Chronicles of the Necromancer,* deals with ghosts, vampires and magic. So, I do a "Days of the Dead International Blog Tour" during the week leading up to Halloween each year. It's a perfect tie-in for me.

You can also invite other experts to be guests on your blog, which increases your traffic. You can comment on news in your industry or trends in publishing. If you write fiction, you can note real-life events that connect with your book or get into detail about topics that relate to your subject, but which you didn't cover in the book itself.

Social Media

Social media includes general sites like Facebook, Twitter, Squidoo, YouTube, LinkedIn, MySpace and other, book-specific sites such as Shelfari, BookMarket.ning.com, AuthorNation, GoodReads, RedRoom, etc. Social media sites are great places for you to reach a global audience that you might not otherwise contact. The key to social media is having good content on your site; updating it frequently; participating by asking and answering questions; hosting virtual events; and being present in the community.

Every time you post to your blog or create a social media site, you become easier to find through search engines, like Google. Google and other search engines look for relevant copy—copy that is on-topic and recent. Every time your name or your book's title comes up in search engine results, it makes it easier for someone to find you and your book.

Plus, search engines really like "inbound links," in other words, links from other sites to yours. When you include links to your home page in your social media text and your blog, you build relevant inbound links, which will also boost your search engine results.

On your social media sites, you can make it easier for readers or prospects to ask you questions, or comment on topics related to your book. You can upload video, audio, or even photos from your recent speaking engagements or events. Using "widgets" (easy applications that are add-ons to the social media page), you can include your blog and Twitter posts so that every time you add to your blog or "Tweet" on Twitter, your Facebook page gets the update—automatically. This adds fresh content without requiring you to go post it to every social media site where you have a profile.

The key with social media is to make sure that you are setting up pages on sites that have already attracted your target audience. If you've written a business book, avoid social media sites that are purely social. Instead, focus on sites with a business angle. If your book is for writers, make sure you are on sites where writers congregate. If you've written a genre novel (mystery, romance, science fiction, fantasy, horror, etc.), find social media sites that focus on that genre. You'll have more success if you go where the target audience has already congregated.

Don't overlook online profiles that go along with your professional memberships. Many clubs and organizations provide a free member profile, along with your other membership benefits. This is a great place to show that you are part of the club community while introducing fellow members to your book and linking them to your website, blog or other social media pages.

Social media is about cultivating relationships, so don't just slap up profiles on a dozen sites and then abandon them. Your best results will come from choosing one to three initial sites. Concentrate on really investing the time needed to reach out to people, answer questions as much as possible, and become a part of the online community. You can always add more sites later. For routine jobs, such as inviting friends, adding press releases or keeping spam cleared away, consider hiring an assistant or intern for a few hours each week.

Media Pitches and Review Copies

Now that you have your media pitch and reviewer letter perfected, it's a good time to start sending those out. Since you're new at this, you may want to start with a manageable number each week, instead of sending dozens of pitches and review copies all at once. This way you can handle the follow-up. Take it in batches and learn as you go. You'll gain confidence and you may get helpful hints from the reviewers and media people who are among your initial contacts. Take all the tips and advice they're willing to offer. Remember that promoting your book is an ongoing learning opportunity.

Gail's Tip

Don't be afraid to ask reporters, TV/radio/podcast hosts and reviewers for recommendations of other people in their industry you should contact. If you do an interview and it goes well, ask the reporter/interviewer to refer you to other interviewers who need a good guest. Always ask for a link to the online version of an interview or review, and be sure to share the link through your blog, website and social media pages. Begin to compile a list of positive comments from book reviewers. This will come in handy later.

Assignment 10: Social Media Opportunities

• Investigate Facebook, Twitter, MySpace, Squidoo and LinkedIn, plus look for specialized sites that appeal to your profession, industry, topic or genre.

• At a minimum, you should create a Facebook page and a Twitter account. Make your screen names straightforward, so it's easy for people to find you.

• Next, find one specialty site and create a page.

• Spend some time reading the rules, browsing other people's pages and reading the discussion threads. Do this to get an idea of what users are talking about, how people engage with one another, and what the etiquette is for each site. It's best to spend some time getting used to a new online community before diving in. This will help you avoid offending anyone or making a faux pas.

• Be sure to find the address of your new profile pages so you can share that through your blog, newsletter and website. Some sites generate a little "button" with your unique page link. These are great visual elements to announce that you're part of the community!

"Been There, Done That" Author Tip:
    "On Amazon use the "Search Inside" feature for people to get free snippets upfront. Offer an affiliate program for your book and services. Contribute to the books of others. Attend as many functions as your time and wallet will allow."

Elinor Stutz, CEO of Smooth Sale, LLC and author of *Nice Girls Do Get the Sale*, www.SmoothSale.net

Chapter 11: *Two Months Until Launch*

Are you excited yet? Your book is soon going to become a reality, and you've got a lot left to do before you're ready for its debut. With just two months to go, you can start putting the tools and resources you've created to good use. Your goals in these last two months before the launch are to create buzz about yourself, your topic and your book, and to "prime the pump" for advance sales. This month, we'll focus on:
- "Push pages"
- Article directories; and
- Press releases.

"Push Pages"

If your book will be carried on Amazon.com and other online booksellers, find out from your publisher when the pre-order link will go live. You can begin selling once readers have a way to order the book. If you are self-publishing, you can create a pre-order button on your website/ shopping cart.

With non-fiction books, one tactic that is becoming common is the idea of a "push page" prior to launch. Using this method is still unusual for fiction books. (That's OK. It means your push page will stand out.) A push page is a web page that *pushes* pre-orders by offering bonus materials as a reward for early commitment. You can see a copy of my push page at TheWinterKingdoms.com. Push pages usually offer extra goodies, such as additional material, audio downloads, or even freebies from other authors.

If you already know other authors who reach your target audience, but with non-competing messages, you can ask if they would like to cross-market with you. You can do this via your push page by asking them to contribute an excerpt, downloadable chapter, quiz, article, discounts on services, etc. Just make sure that you have a way of fulfilling the bonus downloads so that everyone who pre-orders gets the promised reward.

Article Directories

Another way to raise your visibility, and to increase inbound links to your website (which also helps increase your search engine results), is to contribute articles online. You can submit articles to membership sites that you belong to, thereby both enriching the community library and helping to establish yourself as an expert. You can also submit articles to article directory sites, such as eZineArticles.com. Article directories are an easy way for your content to find its way into blogs, newsletters and other sites. You will retain full attribution and gain links to your websites. You can post your articles for free, and anyone who finds your material can use it for free. However, they are required to include your by-line plus a resource box of contact information that points readers back to you. Your article (and contact information) can end up in publications around the world. It's great visibility and it furthers your reputation as an expert.

Don't despair if you write fiction. You can write articles about the business of writing and publishing. There are plenty of publications dedicated to "how-to" articles for the struggling writer. These include topics on everything from grammar, to time management, to financial issues. Don't forget to bookmark your articles on sites like Digg.com and Delicious.com to raise the visibility of your articles and make them easy for others to forward.

Press Releases

Now is the time to put together a press release about your book. You'll create one main release, and then tweak the first paragraph. This will allow you to tailor it specifically for the types of publications you are targeting.

First, let's look at the basics. Think of a press release as an inverted triangle that is wider at the top and tiny at the bottom. Editors tend to cut releases from the bottom up when they are short on space, so your "inverted triangle" means that you want the really important "who, what, when, where, and why" information up at the top.

Your headline and lead sentence should focus on the readers' needs addressed by the book if it is non-fiction ("New Book Helps Single Moms Get Tough with Budgeting"), as opposed to being about you the author ("Jane Doe Announces a New Book"). Your first sentence should hook the reader with what is new, original or offbeat about your book. Follow up with a sentence that gives the book title, release date, publisher and your name as author. In the next paragraph, give a one-line recap of the book's content, focusing on how it solves a problem or introduces a useful process.

If you have a fiction book, your hook will have to focus on what is new and original in the plot. Your one-line recap will be a plot summary. Then, include one sentence that gives your credentials as an author. In the next paragraph, you can have a line or two about any special launch events, media appearances and book tour signings. You should also include a sentence about your publisher and distributor. It is appropriate to mention here whether the book will be available online, in bookstores and/or through your website. If you are self-publishing, do not mention that. (Unfortunately and unfairly, some market stigma still exists about self-publishing.)

Your last paragraph should include your website, push page and contact information so that a store or interested media outlet can contact you. Limit your release to between 200–300 words. (Less than that may not be accepted by some online sites, and more than that can cost you extra money for paid sites.) Keep your sentences short, use active verbs, and keep the focus on what the book delivers for the reader, not on the book itself. When you emphasize your credentials, do it in a way of that shows how your experience can be beneficial to the reader. You should always double-check the release for typos, especially in the phone number and email address.

In order for the media to see your press release as a professional submission, make sure that you use the traditional press release format. Here is an example of the release I used for my novel, Dark Haven.

FOR IMMEDIATE RELEASE
CONTACT: DreamSpinner Communications 704-595-9581

Dark Haven Continues Fantasy Epic with Vampires, Magic and Vengeance

Charlotte, NC—*Dark Haven*, the newest title in author Gail Z. Martin's bestselling Chronicles of the Necromancer series, begins a new chapter in the epic tale of adventurer Jonmarc Vahanian, Lord of Dark Haven, and King Martris Drayke of Margolan.

In *Dark Haven*, the effects of Jared the Usurper's reign of terror strike at the stability of the Winter Kingdoms. Undead forces align against Lord Jonmarc Vahanian of Dark Haven in a struggle for power between mortals and the *vayash moru*. King Martris Drayke prepares for war against rebels still loyal to Jared. Isencroft is on the brink of civil war. Only one thing is certain—the Winter Kingdoms will be changed forever, and innocence is the first casualty.

The Summoner, the first title in the series, sold through four printings in the first year after its release and has returned for additional printings since then. It remained on the Book Sense bestseller list for over 12 weeks, pegged top spots on many other bestseller lists, and garnered high praise from reviewers and readers. *The Blood King*, book two in the series, followed *The Summoner's* strong sales, making its own appearances on bestseller lists in the U.S. and U.K.

Dark Haven is published by Solaris Books, a new UK-based fantasy and science fiction imprint from BL Publishing, the publishing division of industry-leading, tabletop games company, Games Workshop. *The Summoner, The Blood King* and *Dark Haven* are part of The Chronicles of The Necromancer fantasy adventure series distributed in the U.S. by Simon & Schuster. Ms. Martin is handled by the Ethan Ellenberg Literary Agency in New York City. Learn more at www.ChroniclesOfTheNecromancer.com.

When you submit your press release, embed it in the body of your email. Don't attach it as a document. Reporters are leery of opening attachments for fear of computer viruses, and many firewalls won't permit attachments for that reason. Begin building relationships with media contacts by adding a personal note. This should only be a sentence or two at the beginning that genuinely recognizes a recent article written by the reporter. At the end, politely ask them to consider your release.

You can also submit your release online to a variety of free and paid press release distribution services. Paid distribution can range from around $50 to over $600, depending on how well established the site is, and what kind of extras you add. Some of the best-known paid distribution sites include PR Newswire, PR Web and PR Leap. There are also free sites, such as OpenPR.com, 24-7PressRelease.com, 1888PressRelease.com and others. Each site has requirements about the length and content of releases, so make sure that you read the rules to avoid rejection. Distributing your releases online helps to drive traffic to your website and push page. It also is helpful in boosting your search engine results, and creating more buzz about you and your book.

You may also want to email a copy of your press release to bookstores as you set up signings so that their local marketing person can use it in their newsletter. Remember to notify any local media of all signing dates and events. Always send copies to the publications where you currently live, as well as to your hometown, professional association publications, and your alumni magazines. Adjust the wording of the first paragraph so that the reporter knows upfront that this book is from a hometown native, a local author, a member of the professional association, or an alumni of the university.

Assignment 11: Count Down to Launch
• Two months prior to launch, you should order the bookmarks, business cards and posters you've designed from the printer(s) you've researched.
• Send out press releases and review copies. Contact bookstores, as well as upcoming conventions and/or conferences for speaking opportunities.
• Create an account at eZineArticles.com and begin adding article entries.

Gail's Tip
Make notes in your spreadsheet as you interact with media, reviewers and book stores. Note particular likes/dislikes and who is friendly or prickly. If you find a reviewer who only seems to enjoy trashing books, avoid sending your next book. By making notes as you go along, you'll remember this vital information after a year or so passes when you promote your next book.

"Been There, Done That" Author Tip
"Don't invest more in your giveaways than you're going to get from the book financially or emotionally. A friend decided to promote his futuristic romance by putting together clever (and elaborate) goodie bags for a small conference in the Midwest. The conference was so small, the

participants sat at the same tables throughout the three-day event. When the swag was distributed on the final day, the participants at the author's table tore into their bags. They trashed the bags themselves (which boasted the series logo), extracted the small plush toy and candy, and then shoved all the author-branded bookmarks and pens to the middle of the table with the other refuse. The lady sitting next to the author told him, "Why should I take that stuff? I don't know who this [Author Pen Name] is." The irony is, not only was she sitting next to the writer, his pen name was written on his nametag in letters larger than those used for his real name.

Publishers Marketplace not only tracks deals, its book tracker function can help you track and compare your book's standing on multiple lists. It's is the cheapest and most timely way I know to measure the effect of transitory events (e.g., reviews, advertisements, promotional appearances) on book sales. All book reviews drive sales, especially the very good and the very bad. After all, people love watching a train wreck."

Jean Marie Ward, author of *With Nine You Get Vanyr*
http://JeanMarieWard.com

Chapter 12: *One Month Until Launch*

The months right before, during, and immediately after your launch are critical times for your books. Traditional publishing wisdom holds that a book's sales are strongest in the first 90 days. That's the period often used by publishers and bookstores to measure a book's impact. Books that hit bestseller lists usually accomplish that on the strength of their opening weeks. Even if getting onto the bestseller list isn't your priority, bookstores do determine who gets shelf space based on early sales, so anything you can do to front-load your sales helps.

In this chapter, we'll look at several ways to open strongly. This includes utilizing media exposure, using a "street team" for early buzz and, making plenty of well-promoted personal appearances. It also includes getting the word out by piggybacking with bloggers and websites that reach your audience. This month, put your energy into:

- Creating a media blitz;
- Recruiting your street team;
- Posting your tour schedule; and
- Finalizing contest details.

Media Blitz

You've compiled your media list and written a strong press release and media pitch. Now is the time to swing into gear. Send out your pitches and releases approximately four to six weeks prior to your launch date. This gives the media time to cover your story, while still having time to fit you into their schedule. If you send a first slate of releases out six weeks prior to release, follow up with reminders and additional releases every week to stay on the radar.

Radio hosts usually plan their guest appearances a few weeks in advance. But remember, they're busy people. Factor in that you will need to use a tactful combination of emails and phone calls to land your guest slot. Seven or more "touches," or attempts, are often necessary to break through the host's cluttered inbox and get attention.

Remember that radio is an audio medium, so make sure your speaking voice is pitched to avoid squeaks, awkward pauses and obsessive throat-clearing. You may want to practice by having a friend interview you so you can hone your on-air voice. Avoid nervous gestures like pen clicking, tapping fingers or chair swiveling. They'll be heard over the audio connection. Smiling is one of the best things you can do during a radio interview. Why? Smiling makes your voice sound friendlier. It really makes a difference. Always thank your host, and be a polite guest. Have your top three tips written down, because radio interviews are usually only two to three minutes long, so you need to be prepared.

Podcasts work just like radio except that the interview may be longer (up to two hours), and the audience is more defined. You may want to start with interviews that are shorter and move up as you gain confidence. Try to keep it conversational so listeners aren't bombarded with a monologue. Share information that is useful and fun. Avoid the temptation to go on and on about yourself and your book. People only care about your book from the standpoint of what it does for them. Deliver that, and your interview will be a success.

TV requires a visual. What visuals are related to your book? Demonstrations can be very powerful on TV. Depending on the nature of your book, you may have some photos, illustrations or samples/models for "show and tell." For example, a "how-to" book on scrapbooking could use artful layouts to illustrate expertise. A book about how to dress for an interview could use models dressed as the "do" and "don't" examples. Make sure anything you plan to demo has been cleared in advance with the host so that lighting and cameras can be planned. Also, make sure that you keep the time limit in mind. If you don't have any photos or demos, remember that a lively, enthusiastic guest is also a visual. Read up on how to dress for TV, and then let your vibrant personality shine through.

Recruit Your "Street Team"

The idea of a "street team" comes from radio industry. Radio stations frequently have interns saturate a market with flyers and promotional items. Fortunately, you don't have to have the manpower or the budget of a radio station to make the street team concept work for you.

Do you have a handful of good friends and supportive family members?

Who are the people who have read the manuscript before publication? These are your enthusiastic, beta readers. All of these people can be the *street team* core that can help you get the word out about your book, but they need to be trained on how to help.

First, ask your prospective team members if they'd be willing to help out. You can always offer a signed, advance-review copy of the book, a small gift related to your book, or t-shirts. Sometimes, just being "in the know" is enough reward. Next, think about what you need, as well as what is easy and inexpensive for your street team to do. Here are some ideas:

- Ask local bookstores to carry your book and contact you for a signing;
- Request that local library branches purchase your book;
- Drop off bookmarks or flyers at stores and libraries;
- Write early positive reviews of the book on Amazon or their favorite online book seller, relevant blogs, and/or Twitter.
- Put up advertising posters about any upcoming signings or events in their local coffee shops, universities and other gathering places;
- Invite people, especially friends, to your signings;
- Attend your events and be your "plant" to ask questions;
- Call in during your radio interviews with the questions you would love to answer and
- Provide enthusiastic testimonials on your book.

If your friends have been part of the book creation process and have genuinely enjoyed reading it, there's nothing unethical about "seeding" the audience. After all, the whole reason that big companies give out trial sizes and free samples is that people like to talk about what others are talking about. A good street team primes the pump and gets people talking.

Post Your Tour Schedule

You've gone through all the work to set up media interviews, book signings and live events. Make sure everyone knows about them! You can ask whether the radio station/podcast will do advance promotions. Many do. Some bookstores routinely promote upcoming signings with in-store signage. In addition, they solidify their coverage by airing/publishing press releases, and sending newsletters to VIP readers. Conferences and conventions (whether business or genre) usually promote guest authors/ speakers on their website, in both the program and advance PR. On the other hand, some places do advance promotion better than others, and some don't do it at all. Never assume that they'll fill the seats for you.

If the store or conference isn't planning to do a release, you can provide them with the release you are sending out. Make sure to let them know they are welcome to use it on their website or with local media. You can also promote your upcoming appearances on your blog. Also, don't forget to post your schedule on your homepage and on Twitter and to send it to any relevant websites before, during and after your events. Ask your street team to help get the word out any way they can.

Press releases can focus on your tour schedule's events. You can announce the whole schedule, and you can do a short announcement on each event. The media probably won't pick up every event, but odds are good that many of the releases will get coverage. Ask friends who blog to mention your upcoming events if their readers are in your target audience. Make your upcoming events a regular part of your newsletter as your reader base grows. Post it on your Facebook page and on your profile at sites, such as Shelfari.com and RedRoom.com.

When you do an interview, take the opportunity to mention your upcoming events. If you're at a live event, mention a scheduled radio, podcast or TV appearance. You can also post the links to interviews on Twitter, and on your website and blog. Make sure you set Google Alerts to let you know every time your name and book title are posted anywhere on the web. Reposting the links is also a great "thank you" to the interviewer or the event that invited you. They will appreciate the extra traffic to their sites.

Offer a Contest

We all love free stuff. Although you can't buy readers, you can use contests and giveaways to get their attention. Used intelligently and sparingly, contests can be a great way to spice up a radio or podcast interview, or to make a splash with blog and website readers. The best giveaways have a direct tie-in to your book, encourage people to read your book, and don't cost you a lot of money.

Radio hosts and bloggers love giveaways such as free, autographed books and/or t-shirts. These are all relatively cheap for you to provide, especially when compared to the publicity boost giveaways can create. At a live appearance, you can also promote your book through a drawing for autographed books, as well as t-shirts and/or a small gift basket. (Avoid doing a drawing for a signed book at a bookstore signing event. People will tend to put off purchasing to see if they win a free copy. Use a t-shirt or other item instead.) Keep the cost low. I've seen a very nice basket done with a bookmark, coffee mug, wrapped piece of biscotti and $5 Starbuck's gift card. Or, you could use what you already have, and make a prize pack including a t-shirt, and bookmark. The goal is to get people to sign up, thereby providing their email addresses and joining your reader list.

Even better, you could offer a digital bonus, such as something the winner can download. This saves you shipping and handling. Digital bonuses can include extra materials that are not included in the book, a workbook (for a non-fiction book), screensavers or other attractive digital gifts. If your talents extend into music or art, you could even offer a downloadable song or drawing. Just make sure that you own the copyright to use whatever you offer.

Promote your giveaways as often as possible. I was on a live podcast interview where we were giving away a couple of signed books. I posted to Twitter during commercial breaks about being live on the show. Then I asked people to call in and provide the phone number. When someone did call in and win a book because of my Tweets, the host was pleased and amazed. Make sure you send out any prize copies as quickly as possible after the contest.

Gail's Tip

Many readers like signed "book plates." These are stickers with a design or personal message, possibly even a copy of your book cover that you sign and mail to them. These are especially valued by readers who can't get to one of your live events. Book plates are easy to make with your own computer and a color printer plus a package of printer-friendly labels from the office supply store. They only cost pennies apiece.

Assignment 12: Building Your Street Team

• Make a list of the people you can invite to be on your street team, and decide what perks you can offer to thank them.

• Start pitching the media and making the follow-up calls and emails to get booked.

• Think of what you can offer as a giveaway that is both appealing and inexpensive.

"Been There, Done That" Author Tip

J.C. Hutchins, author of *7ᵗʰ Son: Descent* and *Personal Effects: Dark Art*, relies on his street team to help him introduce his podcasts and books to newcomers. He even supplies them with a special "widget" that they can add to the websites, blogs, MySpace/Facebook pages or forums that they frequent. The widget is offered to anyone who clicks through a link, and provides plenty of promos, pictures and more. It's like a push page in a link. Hutchins ran a contest to see who could get the most views from the link, and gave away free t-shirts as a reward. He sends his dedicated street team on monthly missions with clear objectives, fun rewards, and the tools they need to do the job. http://jchutchins.net

Chapter 13: *Launch!*

Congratulations, your book is now available! Celebrate seeing your new book on bookstore shelves, and give yourself a well-deserved reward. While the hard work of creating the book may be over, the challenge of promoting your book is just beginning a new phase.

Launch month is a crucial time for visibility. It's also when you see all your prior efforts begin to pay off as you make use of the tools you've created. Your launch is the perfect time to redouble your efforts to make personal connections with readers to create relationships, as well as sales. Your focus this month should be:

- Making the most of your signings and events; and
- Remaining visible.

Signings and Events

Now that your book is in stores, your launch month should include as many weekend book signings as your schedule will permit. Book signings are important for several reasons. First, they give the store a reason to draw attention to your book, and they help establish your reputation as an author.

Readers enjoy the opportunity to meet an author and ask questions. Know that until you have a well-established fan base on several books, few of the questions you'll get from readers will be about your own work. Most questions tend to be about the genre or topic of discussion, or about publishing. Don't be disappointed that the focus isn't on your books. When the conversation centers on your topic or genre, you have the opportunity to gently demonstrate your expertise (avoid the temptation to lecture). And, when the questions focus on how to break into publishing, provide helpful tips and encouragement, and be grateful that you have reached a point in your own publishing success where others want your advice.

Whether you speak at book clubs, genre events (such as romance or science fiction conventions), or at scholarly or industry conferences, remember that your speaking engagements will not really be about your book. You will be primarily asked to speak on topics related to the subject of your book. However, don't mistake this as an invitation to do an infomercial. If you make the speech into a sales pitch, you will lose the chance to demonstrate your credibility and to forge a bond with the audience. Instead, whether your book is fiction or non-fiction, focus on being entertaining, accessible, and down-to-earth. Also, always provide your listeners with useful nuggets of information.

Never forget to take copies of your books with you to the speaking engagements you do that are not in bookstores. Many panelists at genre conventions will place at least one copy of their various books on the table in front of them. This gives listeners a visual reminder of the titles they have written. Bring business cards and bookmarks to hand out to attendees. You can even offer a downloadable bonus item, such as a free chapter, an audio file, or extended material on your website. This will also drive extra online traffic and build your reader list.

Reference your book when you speak, but don't withhold information. Give a quick, detailed overview of something in your book and mention that you provide more in-depth information in the book. Don't try to blackmail listeners by insisting that they buy your book in order to get any useful information. Your "free samples" of the story or topic should be strong enough to entice them to buy the book on their own.

Fiction authors often get the chance to do a short reading from their books. This is especially true at genre-specific events and book-club meetings. Plan for this in advance by choosing a passage that will grab their interest. Many writers start with the beginning of their first chapter, but only do this if time permits for you to read far enough for it to be engaging and make sense. Otherwise, pick a dramatic action passage that doesn't give away the plot, but still demonstrates characterization or tone. Read the passage aloud to practice, and time yourself. Most readings should last only five minutes or less, unless you are a master vocal dramatist. You can also use a program like AudioAcrobat.com to record yourself as you read, and then make the audio available via your website.

Always ask before each speaking engagement to find out whether you are permitted to have a table in the back of the room to sell your books and other materials. If you're self-published, you probably have enough books to easily stock the table. You may not have a supply of books to sell if you are traditionally published and distribute through bookstores. That's ok. You can autograph bookmarks, or give away excerpts from your book on CD or in print. You may also have a laptop with an Internet connection so that you can sell books via Amazon or another online bookstore live at the event.

Or, you may have related materials such as home study courses, coaching cards, calendars, t-shirts or other tie-in items. Even if you have nothing to sell, a table in the back can reinforce your author credentials. A poster-sized display of your book cover, plus business cards and bookmarks, makes a great way to make sure that your book is remembered. Remember to include your website and ISBN number on all your promotional materials.

Remaining Visible

Launch month is a great time to throw a launch party at a bookstore or a conference where you'll be appearing. This is usually as simple as bringing a large sheet cake with punch, cookies, crackers and a cheese tray. Make sure that you display your book while you meet and greet. If you have the time, some bakeries can "print" your book cover graphic (using a computer file) directly on the top of the cake, using a special printer with food coloring ink.

If your pre-launch promotion efforts included contests and giveaways, make sure you honor the obligation and send signed copies to the winners. Avoid doing a drawing for a free book at bookstore events because it tends to depress sales. People usually want to see whether they've won a free book before paying for one themselves.

Update your online social information daily by adding posts on your blog, Twitter, website, Facebook or other pages. Let people know about how actively you're making personal appearances. Make positive comments on meeting and greeting readers and bookstore personnel.

PR shouldn't stop with the announcement of your launch. Once you've announced that the book is available, keep up a steady stream of PR by announcing upcoming appearances, contests, online events, and other related news. If you are considered for an award, just making the short list is newsworthy, even if you don't win. And of course, if you do win an award, send out a release to let the world know!

Consider reaching out to book clubs as another way to increase your visibility. There are book clubs and literature discussion groups in every city and many small towns. You can find them by asking bookstore managers and librarians, doing Internet searches, and checking out sites like MeetUp.com. Write up a study guide for your book that includes questions for discussion, and make it available as a free download on your website. Remember, you can participate *live* with study groups in distant cities by doing a call via speakerphone or webcam. Then begin to contact book clubs to see if they will invite you as a speaker. Some clubs focus on only certain types of books, so your book won't suit everyone. However, book clubs can be a great way to spread the buzz about your book with dedicated readers.

Be visible in forums and chat rooms online. Answer questions related to your topic or genre on highly-trafficked blogs, membership sites and forum boards. Always include a signature file that has your name, website, book title, Twitter address and email so people can find your book.

Launch month is when you need your street team more than ever. Supply them with review copies early and ask them to blog about the book or to post comments on Amazon and other bookseller sites. Have them make a point of asking librarians and bookstore managers to stock your book. Give them downloadable flyers or mail them bookmarks so they can drop them off at local bookstores or coffee houses. Most importantly, encourage your street team to talk about your book to their friends, both live and online. Even a handful of enthusiastic early readers can make a big splash when it comes to generating excitement.

Assignment 13: 3-2-1 Launch!
- Make sure your social media sites are set up and prepped, then set aside time to be very visible.
- Prepare to sparkle on your interviews and live events. If that requires large amounts of caffeine, so be it.
- Reframe your attitude to make publicity is a joy instead of a chore. You are a writer! Celebrate by enjoying the live and online social life that goes with it (aka promotion).

"Been There, Done That" Author Tip
"Early on in writing your book, I recommend that you create and begin to implement your strategic plan for marketing. Create a vision, purpose,

and mission statement for your book, then develop the strategies and finally the tasks to begin to attain that vision. This plan will be a critical component of your book proposal to publishers, or if self-publishing, a guide to help you through the maze. Once you know the why and how of what you want to accomplish, the Law of Attraction is activated and the Universe opens up. Obstacles will arise, but having a specific target and the plan to move beyond those hurdles is critical. As you create your vision, look at your marketing efforts as a way to enlighten others by helping them with new perspectives, experiences, and knowledge. Make the offering of your book more fun by taking the emphasis off of the "sale" and putting it on how your writing will help others by the information and guidance you provide, and the stories you share."

Marilyn Schwader, author of *The Guide to Getting It: Branding and Marketing Mastery* www.ClarityOfVision.com.

Chapter 14: *Launch Plus One Month*

Are you still excited about being an author? That's good, because your work isn't done. The month after your launch is still a crucial part of the 90-day period when bookstores and publishers are closely watching sales. It's important to maximize your visibility while your new book is still *new*. So, drink some more coffee—there's still more to do!

Your goals this month will be:
- Building connections with other authors
- Using social media to keep buzz going
- Catching up on important tasks

Build Connections

Hanging out with other authors is one of the coolest things that an author gets to do. They are your best source for new promotional ideas and opportunities to collaborate on new projects. These relationships can also help you contribute to upcoming anthologies and magazines. They're also your best way to hear news about your industry. Make the most of any opportunity you have to get to know other authors, both in your genre and outside of your topic.

Borrow promotional ideas from what's being done in other types of writing. For example, push pages are common for non-fiction, but less frequently done in genre fiction. I borrowed the idea and created a very successful push page for one of my recent novels. Everyone remarked on how unusual it was, making it newsworthy. That gave it extra attention.

Other authors also are a great source of information and encouragement. The writing world is relatively small, so remember that you are probably only one or two degrees of separation from others and act accordingly. Think twice before saying anything negative, and ask around if there's another author you need to meet. Odds are good someone you know already knows that person and can connect you.

Getting to know other authors is also a great way to build a network that can recommend media contacts, agents, editors and printers. You can find out about scams, and get tips on great deals. Once you get to know other authors in your genre or field, you can ask them to write a cover blurb or offer to do the same for them. You can cross-promote each other by guest blogging or by Tweeting news and links. (A "Tweet" is a single message on Twitter.)

There are other practical reasons to get to know other authors. Going to conventions and conferences gets expensive. As you get to know other authors, you can share rides, share hotel rooms, even split the cost of supplies. You can do joint readings to attract larger audiences, and share the cost of a table in the dealer's room (as well as giving each other back-up table coverage that's long enough for meals and bathroom breaks). Writing is a solitary profession. Only other writers really understand the frustration of writer's block. It's great to be able to fire off an email or a direct Tweet to a friend who can Tweet back with words of encouragement.

How do you get to know other authors? Attend their book signings. For best results, start off by picking authors who are also just getting started. Introduce yourself, exchange business cards, and chat about their book. Then, it's a good idea to "Tweet" about meeting them, and give them a plug about their book tour. I've found that being the first to give, and do so generously, is a great way to make a connection. If you hit it off, offer to have them as a guest on your blog or on your podcast. Most people will make an offer in return. Now, you're cross-promoting.

At conferences and conventions, hang out in the "green room" author lounge. Strike up conversations, but don't be pushy. Always make the conversation about them, by asking questions about their newest book, tour, panels, and future plans. Don't worry! Most people will get around to asking you about your projects as well. Within genres and industries, authors tend to cross paths a lot. That's why you can never have too many friends, and one enemy is one too many. Go out of your way to be polite and don't hold a grudge. The person who seemed to brush you off may have been jetlagged, getting over the flu or sleep deprived.

When you're on a panel with other authors, make a point of exchanging business cards. Don't forget to drop them a line after the event to say how nice it was to meet them. Invite them to follow you on Twitter and do the same. Post a nice comment on their blog about how great it was to meet them, and how much fun the event was. Connect authors with other resources you can recommend. Everyone likes the person who always adds value. Talk up other people's books and re-Tweet their comments. Bookmark their articles to social tagging sites like Digg.com. In other words, don't be afraid to be a friend. People notice.

Update Your Social Media Sources

For writers, building an audience on social media sites like Facebook and Twitter isn't just a numbers game. Yes, there are techniques and add-on programs that can amass huge numbers of friends and followers, but few of the people added that way will ever buy your book.

A better way is to build your list organically. That means encouraging your readers to follow or friend you by inviting them through your blog, newsletter and personal appearances. Twitter writing tips or even the first chapter of your book. "Follow" (add as a friend) your fellow authors and the thought-leaders in your industry, and then follow their top followers (presuming that their followers share an interest in the topic). Join Facebook groups and Twitter Twibes (Twibes.com) that focus on your genre or topic and invite people to follow/friend you. It's easier to spend the elbow grease to *follow* and *friend* the right people than to unfollow thousands of people who will never be your audience.

The same goes for the conventional wisdom that you must Tweet and blog obsessively in order to build an audience. While you should update regularly and relatively frequently, most authors have a goal of reaching out to their audience, rather than building a huge base as an end in itself. I'd much rather get Tweets and messages that actually have interesting content than a stream of junk, and I suspect so would your real prospects. Twitter once a workday or at least a few posts every couple of days. Try to blog once a week. Remember, some of those posts can be about upcoming or just-finished events, and can boost the other authors you meet. Avoid posts that are only continuous self-promotion. Throw in interesting quotes, links to videos, and fun facts, as well as useful tips.

Do Your Housekeeping

If you haven't already announced your contest winners, now is a good time to do that. Respect privacy and use only initials and a hometown, or just first names. Avoid giving out any contact information or personal data. If you've awarded a prize in person, you can post a photo of the contest winner, or a webcam video, with their permission.

Post the links to your most recent press releases, interviews and podcast segments. As you amass more of these, create a Press Page to maintain a record of your appearances for the media and interested fans once the information is no longer newsworthy enough for your home page. On your press page, you can also have a Press Kit with your bio, a fact sheet about your book, and a growing list of reviewer comments and reader raves.

Keep generating ideas for new articles, based on your book and new media pitches. This element of promotion is never over. If you have a good non-fiction title, you can stay media-worthy forever by tying your expertise to hot headlines. For fiction, maintaining an active tour schedule and a vibrant website can help you stay in the news. Welcome invitations from others to contribute to author surveys, start your own podcast, learn to create webcam videos, and post them to YouTube. All of these are great ways to stay visible after the first rush of publicity.

Nourish Your Street Team

In order to keep your street team, you'll need to give them ways to stay involved. Make them feel they are making a contribution without asking for too much. You also need to reward them with first access, and give them juicy new information before the public whenever possible.

Engage your street team by inviting them to your live events, and asking for their help to Tweet and post updates. You need all the help you can get. Ask for their ideas on what kinds of things they'd like to do. Not only does asking for input help your team feel valued, you are likely to get great ideas you hadn't thought of before. Ask them whether they know any book clubs or on-campus groups that might need a speaker. Also, see if they can recommend podcasts, bloggers or websites you might not have found yet. Find out what sites they are visiting on the Internet, what blogs they read, who they follow on Twitter, and then do likewise.

Your street team can also be your eyes and ears. What do they see other authors doing that is cool? What isn't working? Don't be afraid to draw promotional ideas from musicians, artists and others who are pushing the envelope in terms of visibility. Odds are your street team members have eclectic tastes and may be aware of trends you don't see. Ask for their help!

Some additional ways to keep your street team active is by keeping them supplied with seasonal posters and new promotional items. If your street team is made up of avid readers, it probably isn't a hardship to give them a reason to visit their favorite bookstore every few months. If someone posts a particularly negative review on a website or a nasty comment on an online bookstore site, ask someone from your street team if they're comfortable writing a positive note to help offset any negativity. Be sincere, prompt and effusive in your thanks.

Gail's Tip

Handle your street team with care. They are golden!

Assignment 14: Managing Your Success

• Compile a monthly list of the press releases, podcast and interview links so you can easily update your website and post the links to bookmarking sites.

• Be on the lookout for what other authors are doing—both within your industry/genre, and in totally unrelated areas. A good idea deserves to be adapted and copied.

• Take a look at the guest roster for any upcoming conferences and conventions you are attending. Make a note of the other authors, and start visiting their sites so that you can strike up an intelligent conversation about their work. Begin building bridges.

"Been There, Done That" Author Tip:

"Don't try to sell the book. Try to sell yourself. I tell people to come in and meet the author. I'm a funny guy. I'm wonderful to know. Did I say anything about money? Meet the author. An individual book is not the product. You're the product. Never lie. Never mislead. Tell the truth and readers will trust you. You want them to come back."

C.J. Henderson, author of *The Things that Are Not There*. www.cjhenderson.com

Chapter 15: *Launch Plus Two Months*

Are you feeling more like a "real" author? As you can see, it's not quite as glamorous as the TV shows make it out to be, what with schlepping your books and promotional materials around in your trunk, spending hours uploading press releases, and sending out media pitches.

Mom was right. Things that are worthwhile are worth working for, and that includes your writing career. I want to share some additional tools and tricks to use during this crucial launch month to help you lessen the burden. I will also give you other ideas for extending your promotion, including:

- Virtual assistants
- Easy tech additions

I coulda' had a VA

No, not a vegetable drink or a government department, but a Virtual Assistant (VA). Virtual assistants are people with administrative and web skills who help you with the kinds of things we've been doing in this book: posting press releases, researching media, building your reviewer list, updating your website, *friending* and *following* likely prospects on Facebook, Twitter and elsewhere, and other essential tasks. They are "virtual" because they don't work from your home or office. Instead, they work from wherever they are located, and stay in touch with you via the web and email. They may literally be on the other side of the world, or just across town.

I don't think it's a bad idea to do these tasks yourself at first, for a couple of reasons. You need to understand the process to know the time, effort and skills involved before you can hire someone else. You also benefit from doing some of the initial research yourself, so that you understand how your own promotion works. (After all, even a great VA may be temporarily unavailable, and you will have to do for yourself.) Doing these tasks yourself at first also helps you to identify where your own strengths and weaknesses are so you can delegate your weak spots and keep the areas that benefit from your personal touch.

You can find VAs on sites like Elance.com, Guru.com and Craigslist. There are also programs that train VAs to work with authors and some VAs who specialize in helping authors.

Before you contact a VA, think about a list of tasks you might have that person start with, and what it will take for them to do the tasks successfully. This is where it really helps to have done the task first yourself. Think about how much money you can afford to spend. This will determine the number of hours you will be able to pay for. Also think about the sets of skills your tasks will require: using specific computer programs, familiarity with the Internet or with web programming, attention to detail, fluency in English, etc.

Be willing to divide the tasks up to get the best deals and the best skill sets. You may find that by having several part-time VAs you can control your costs. In addition, you can use people who are experts at a certain kind of task, without requiring someone be a jack-of-all-trades. Tasks that are fairly routine, or that are programming-based, can even be offshored. When you post your job description on a site like Elance, you will receive bids from providers all over the world. Review their feedback and portfolios carefully, and don't be afraid to ask questions. If you find a provider you like, but whose price isn't what you hoped, contact them and see if you can work out the difference.

I have used Elance successfully for several years to help me create slides for speaking engagements, and to create web graphics for my podcast sites. I've also hired VAs to upload my press releases online, add events to event calendars, format my newsletters, and help with media and reviewer research. VAs can also help you keep up with your social media sites by posting blog entries or Tweets you've written on a regular schedule, cleaning off inappropriate comments from your Facebook page comments section, or updating your online events calendars, and inviting new friends or followers based on your criteria. All of this frees you to write, create, network with other authors, and do the kinds of promotion that requires your personal presence.

Explore Easy Tech Additions
The market is now full of inexpensive digital video cameras specially

made for easy web uploading. If you haven't explored digital video cameras yet, this is a good time to try one out. Think of all the ways you can use web video to liven up your website, add interest to your blog, and extend your online visibility. There are sure to be new cameras coming out all the time. Do your research, and be sure it's very easy to upload digital video from the camera you buy.

Non-fiction authors can create short (under five minute) video blogs of themselves that provide tips based on the book or body of knowledge. Fiction authors can videoblog from conventions and events or just record themselves musing about topics of interest to readers. Realize that would-be writers are also a potential audience. They are hungry for insight into the writing life, which is another great topic to explore. Once you have your video, upload it to YouTube, and share it with the world.

You can also use AudioAcrobat.com to make it easier to share your videos by creating easy-to-email links or videoplayers for the web. AudioAcrobat also makes another great promotional opportunity easy: podcasting.

Podcasts are similar to radio shows, only with an audience segmented by topic or interest, rather than music type or geography. You can create podcasts about your area of expertise, if you are a non-fiction author, or about your genre, if you write fiction. Mur Lafferty, a very successful podcaster and author of *Playing for Keeps*, hosts the *I Should Be Writing* podcast about….things that distract her from writing. Podcasting is a great way to extend your voice and reach a new audience.

I host the *Shared Dreams Podcast* (SharedDreamsPodcast.com), where I interview experts who are relevant to authors and small business owners. I also host the *Ghost in the Machine Podcast* (GhostInTheMachinePodcast.com) featuring authors of fantasy, science fiction and paranormal books. Doing the podcasts has helped me meet new people, make great connections, and encourage cross promotion. I blog and promote the show about these experts/authors (which introduces my readers to them), and they blog and promote about being on the show (which introduces their readers to me).

Another type of podcasting includes creating audio or dramatic versions of your book. Podiobooks.com is a leading site. Authors such as J.C. Hutchins, Christiana Ellis, Scott Sigler and Mur Lafferty got a start there. The idea behind creating a podcast of your book is similar to the old radio serials. You break your book up either by scenes or chapters, and then either read aloud or get some friends to help you dramatize the book. While a good podcast requires learning to use some new equipment, the cost is minimal and the programs are easy to use. The great part about creating a "podiobook" is that it introduces new readers to you at a point in your career when you may not yet be commercially attractive to the big audio book creation services, which demand a certain level of book sales. You can choose to charge for your audio book downloads, give them away (research suggests that this increases book sales rather than decreasing them), or offer readers the choice to contribute what they want for the download.

You can begin podcasting with AudioAcrobat, using nothing but a landline phone with a clear connection and a good Internet connection. AudioAcrobat includes the ability to upload your podcast to iTunes and create an RSS feed, which lets listeners subscribe to your "show." If you decide that you want to get more serious about podcasting, specialized recording equipment is still relatively inexpensive, and the podcasting community is extremely helpful. Check out Tee Morris's *Podcasting for Dummies* for more details.

Don't overlook the power of photos. Digital cameras make taking and uploading photos simple and free. With a site like Flickr.com, you can upload photos from your travels, signings and events, as well as create fun and easy slide shows. You can use photos and easy-to-use software like Microsoft® Movie Maker® and similar programs to create your own book video. Just make sure that the images and music you use are either your own creation, or obtained from a royalty-free site.

For a more professional book video, consider having a professional create what is essentially a thirty- to sixty-second web commercial for your book. Circle of Seven (COS Productions) trademarked the concept of a "book trailer" (akin to a movie trailer), and pioneered the idea. I used Circle of Seven to create my book video, and it has not only gotten thousands of views, but it has also helped to create media buzz. Your book video becomes a digital calling card. You can post it on your website, include a link to it in your email signature, blog about it, "Tweet" it, and show it on your laptop during book signings.

Explore Your Subsidiary Rights
Of course, this month you'll still be following up with reporters and

reviewers, pitching new stories, uploading articles and keeping your social media sites fresh. It's also a great time to explore the ways you can create additional information products that go beyond your book.

Start by looking at the contract you have with your publisher if you are traditionally published. Who controls the rights to ebooks, audiobooks, and tie-in products? If you're not sure, ask your agent. If you self-published, the good news is that you control all rights.

Think about the tie-in products that go along with any major movie— posters, calendars, action figures, trading cards, mugs, t-shirts...the list seems endless. While you may not be ready to be an action figure, look around your local bookstore and you'll see that plenty of authors now sell more than books.

If you have a how-to book, does it lend itself to a video series? A cookbook can become a "how-to" video. An exercise book can become a thirty-minute workout DVD. Almost any subject can become an audio file or CD for people who would rather listen while they travel. You may be able to take a memorable line from your books (look into trademarking it!) and use it on t-shirts, coffee mugs, computer mouse pads and other items. Thought-a-day calendars are also popular, especially for self-help subjects. "Coaching cards" are decks of cards with key concepts, quotes, or thoughts from your books that a reader can draw from each day to meditate on an important concept.

Author Kevin J. Anderson was among the first to create a CD of original music to accompany his books. Anderson says his music isn't meant to be a soundtrack; rather, it can be enjoyed independent of the book but takes on more meaning for those who have read the novel. While you may not be up to creating a rock CD, what about a CD of meditations, guided imagery or one-minute daily tips and motivations?

Think outside the book. An exercise book may lead to a cookbook of healthy recipes. A self-help book could lead to a branded journal for readers to record their personal struggles and triumphs. J.F. Lewis, author of *Staked* and *Revamped*, has turned a t-shirt from a fictional music event in his books into a promotional item he offers for sale.

Assignment 15: Getting the Most from a VA

• Compile a list of the tasks you would ultimately like to outsource to a Virtual Assistant. Group the tasks according to common skills required, and write up a description of what you would like to have done along with the skills needed. Determine a monthly budget and when you are ready to commit. Post your project online to find qualified help.

• Explore ways to create a multimedia experience using videoblogging, web video and web audio. Find out whether podcasting or audio books are right for you, and learn more about book videos.

• Whether or not you're ready to take the step right now, start thinking about how you might create information products or tie-ins based on your book. Keep your eyes open when you're in bookstores to see what other authors are doing. Make a list of the merchandising that goes along with blockbuster novels and hit movies.

"Been There, Done That" Author Tip:

"Reach out to your fellow professionals. Most of them remember what it was like to be where you are and many are more than willing to help spread the word about your book. When John Scalzi featured STAKED in the Big Idea feature on his "Whatever" blog, I had a noticeable increase in hits on my website and a distinct spike in my Amazon numbers. But be polite. If they don't have the time to help you this time around, don't take it personally. Be courteous and move on to the next idea."

J. F. Lewis, author of *Staked* and *Revamped* http://authoratlarge.com.

Chapter 16: *Launch Plus Three Months*

By now, book promotion should start to feel more comfortable as you get more used to your role as author. You've also realized that as time goes on, much of your promotion will be more of the same. There will be scheduling and performing at book signings, conferences, speaking engagements and events; pitching and following up with the traditional and online media; keeping your website and social media sites fresh; and being visible on Twitter and in online forums or chats.

Since your book isn't exactly "new" anymore, how do you stay in demand as a media guest? The answer is by being a great interviewee that is fun to have on the show, full of useful/entertaining information that gets readers/listeners to comment, and who is polite and easy to get along with. You can generate more interest by finding new connections between your content and the most recent headlines in the news.

This month, let's look at some other ways to extend your book and your platform:

• Creating your own teleseminars, workshops and live events, or co-creating programs and promotions with other authors or thought leaders;

• Reformatting your book as an e-book; and

• Exploring non-bookstore opportunities.

Creating or Co-creating Events

Creating seminars or workshops based on the material in your book may be easier for non-fiction authors, but fiction authors aren't necessarily sidelined. Coaches, consultants and experts usually have a wealth of knowledge beyond what is in their books. Fiction authors also have experience they can share information on the business of being a writer, writing tips for not-yet-published writers, or interesting information from their research or area of speciality. This is important, because readers often want the opportunity to customize what they've discovered in your book by working directly with the author. Teleseminars, webinars, workshops and live events are a natural progression.

Teleseminars are the easiest and most cost-effective option, because they require only a good phone connection and a way to have multiple callers at one time. Programs like FreeConference.com make it easy to have up to 100 people on the line. A teleseminar consists of only you and your information, but you have the opportunity to take questions, and the audience can add comments.

A webinar offers the opportunity to have a slide show along with your voice. There are many webinar platforms, but GoToWebinar.com™ is one of the easiest for beginners. A webinar is more complex, but it also includes more capabilities, such as polling to do surveys during the program, and the ability to use a shared whiteboard.

The great part with teleseminars and webinars is that you don't have to incur the risk of contracting for space and food at a hotel, especially if you aren't certain of the turnout for an event. Your attendees can participate from their desks, meaning they don't have to take the time or expense to commute or park. And, you can record both teleseminars and webinars to allow attendees to time-shift, or to create an additional infoproduct from the recording.

When you're a new expert, it's easiest to offer teleseminars and webinars by giving a presentation for an online group that has an established following because you probably don't have the following yet to create enough traffic and attendance for a stand-alone program. Look for organizations, websites and membership groups that offer teleseminars or webinars, and find out how they choose their speakers, and then offer to present a program for them. Some places pay presenters and some don't. Initially, your biggest goal is visibility for you as an expert and for your book, so don't worry too much about getting paid right away unless you are already a very established speaker.

It can be easier to draw a crowd if you collaborate with another expert author, or thought leader. This is because now you can cross-promote the event to both of your reader mailing lists, and reach double the number of people. Just make sure that you and your co-presenter have worked out the roles/responsibilities and cost/profit sharing in writing ahead of time.

Explore E-books
Many readers like the convenience of being able to load hundreds of

books onto an e-reader device like Amazon's Kindle, especially if they travel. Be warned that creating an e-book is more than just making your book available in PDF format. E-readers have a variety of formats, and producing a book that is compatible with their formatting and is also well-designed is best left to a professional.

Check to see whether you or your publisher control e-publishing rights. If you control the rights, ask other authors for recommendations of publishers who specialize in e-books, and find out which authors are pleased with the production quality, promotion and distribution of their e-books. Avoid the temptation to just download an e-book creator program from the Internet. The results are unlikely to be professional in the hands of a first-time user. If your publisher controls the rights, ask politely but repeatedly, until you get them to create an e-book version of your book. It's a growing market, and you won't want to miss out.

Non-bookstore Sales

Bookstores aren't the only places people buy books. Books are for sale in sporting goods stores, gift shops, baby stores, New Age shops, specialty-interest stores, religious stores and other non-bookstore shops. Books are also sold through catalogs, and tens-of-thousands of books are given away by corporations as gifts or premiums. Not only can you reach a whole new audience through non-bookstore sales, but the profit margin and return policies of these alternative distribution outlets can often be more favorable than traditional bookstores.

How do you find these outlets? Dan Poynter's ParaPublishing.com offers lists for sale. You can also build your own list. It takes some sleuthing to find the contact for the buyer, and it may require a trip to the trade shows where stores purchase their inventory. However, the results can be profitable if your book finds a perfect distribution outlet.

Locally, you can do the legwork yourself and get a feel for what buyers want, and what questions you'll face. You'll need to do this level of selling personally, not via mass email or letters. On the other hand, there are plenty of success stories attesting to authors who sold thousands of their books in a single order to a catalog or a corporate buyer, so the rewards can be worth the effort.

Gail's Tip

Don't be afraid to ask questions. Find out who handles the e-books or audio books for other authors you meet. Ask authors of related but non-competing books for non-bookstore marketing contacts. And, of course, be willing to share your knowledge with other authors. What goes around comes around!

Assignment 16: Setting Out on New Ventures

• Brainstorm topics for possible teleseminars or webinars based on your book. Google to see what the competition is for those topics.

• Start jotting down ideas for non-bookstore sales opportunities. Find a few outlets in your area and make contact. Learn from the experience and apply what you've discovered to make new sales.

• See how many of the authors in your niche have e-books or audio books. Which electronic or audio publisher are they using? Check out those publishers to see what types of books they handle. Be sure to ask questions when you talk with other authors.

"Been There, Done That" Author Tip

"For my WVMP Radio urban fantasy series, I have a set of amazing volunteers called a Street Team (after the posses who help spread the word for real radio stations and bands). I send them bookmarks to distribute to booksellers, librarians, family and friends. They add my specially designed widgets and playlists to their blogs, MySpace, Facebook pages, etc. They blog or Twitter about new releases, write reviews, recruit newsletter subscribers, and more. Many of them are much more outgoing than I am, and they've convinced bookstores and libraries to order my books. I don't know what I would do without them!"

Jeri Smith-Ready, author of *Wicked Game* and *Bad to the Bone*
www.JeriSmithReady.com.

Chapter 17: *Launch Plus Four Months*

Probably by now, you've figured out that the easy part about being an author is writing the book. The hard part is creating the visibility for your book so that plenty of people know it exists in order to buy it. The best book in the world will just sit on the shelf, unless readers know it's there. And that, dear author, is your job, as you've learned. This is a good time to:

• Do some housekeeping, based on your book reviews and feedback, to make sure you're ready for the opportunities that come your way;

• Prepare for new live events; and

• Explore seasonal or gift "hooks" for your book.

Making the Most of Reviews

Compile a list of your best reviews and post it on your site. Create a short list of your best reviews and add it to your press kit. You'll want to use this list of review quotes the next time you prepare a proposal. This is important whether the proposal is for the next book in your series, or for a completely different book. Why? Because reviewer quotes help to boost your credibility as a successful writer.

Reviews are often far too long to quote in their entirety. It's accepted practice to select an excerpt that praises your book. Make sure you attribute the review by citing the name of the publication and the reviewer, if known. To avoid copyright problems, it's better to link to a full review from your site, rather than copying or pasting it onto your site.

You may find that your book is reviewed by people to whom you never sent a review copy, and may not be reviewed by publications which did receive a book. Make notes on where your reviews are appearing. For the next book, contact the reviewers who wrote reviews on your initial book. Sending out advance review copies is expensive. It makes sense to send them where they stand the most chance of being read.

Today, your book is more likely to be reviewed by "citizen journalists" rather than by the professional reviewers at big newspapers or magazines.

That's fine. Many of these "amateur" reviewers do so out of love for books and a particular genre. They are probably more in touch with the average reader's taste than some professionals. Treat every reviewer with respect. Thank them by sending an email, or posting a comment on the blog. When the next book rolls around, find out how to contact the reviewers and ask if they would be willing to review your new book. Odds are in your favor. Plus, these citizen-reviewers tend to have a small, but loyal, readership who can be great opinion leaders to help you generate early buzz. Make sure your reviewer spreadsheet remains up to date.

Prepare for Events

Take a look at your live events to see where you need to reorder materials, create new posters, or add something new, like a specialized handout based on your book. Now that you're more comfortable in front of an audience, you may want to get a professional video done of you at a speaking engagement. Ask around. It's possible to find professional videographers who offer extremely reduced rates for weekday shoots. Take a look at the videos of other authors, coaches, speakers or consultants, who target the same audience as you do, to get an idea what the standard is. Your videographer will need to see the best of these sites in order to know what style you want for your video.

You can also use your digital video camera to get videos for your panels, or more casual presentations. While these can be great for promotion, you can also learn a lot by watching yourself present and looking for ways to improve your delivery, appearance or mannerisms. Even the top pros watch videos of themselves, just like athletes, looking for ways to improve. It's like having a free speaking coach.

If you aren't satisfied with your performances, consider retaining a professional speaking coach for a few sessions, to help you polish your delivery. It's amazing what a good coach can help you achieve in a short period of time. With a speaking coach, you won't just see areas where you could be better. You'll also get good advice on what to do differently, which can improve both your performance and your confidence. As a professional who will depend on public appearances for part of your livelihood, it can be a very worthwhile investment.

Seasonal Tie-ins and Gift Opportunities

Experts say that most book buyers are women, and bookstore managers will tell you that a large number of books are given as gifts. Once your book is no longer new, you'll need to find ways to keep it in the news. Two of the best ways are by looking for seasonal hooks and positioning your book for the female and gift-buying markets.

How do you create a seasonal or gift hook? Look for a natural connection. New Year's resolutions, and the months just before bathing suit season, are great times to promote books on fitness or losing weight. Mothers' Day is a perfect time for books on family history, crafts, memoirs, poetry or gentle humor. Graduation can be a wonderful opportunity for motivational or career books, books on how to dress for the workplace, or on starting a small business. Summer and early fall are popular times for weddings, creating a great connection for how-to guides for catering or cake decorating, manner and etiquette manuals, travel planners, and gift books suitable for new couples, or for members of the wedding party.

It's up to you to pitch your book for seasonal and gift opportunities. Three to six months prior to the holiday or season, create a press release and a new pitch focused on the hook. Contact media that focus on the particular tie-in event (bridal publications, travel magazines, career sites, etc.), and promote yourself as an expert and your book as a resource. Do the same with bookstore managers and offer to do an in-store workshop or demonstration around the season/holiday.

You'll use a similar approach with non-bookstore outlets such as catalogs and gift stores, but give yourself more time. Approach these venues at least six months to a year in advance. You can also look for local expos for women, brides, new graduates, job hunters, craft enthusiasts or genre readers, and use your seasonal pitch tweaked with special emphasis for that particular target group.

When it comes to holidays, realize that our diverse society has new opportunities beyond birthdays and Christmas. Especially in metropolitan areas, you'll see a spectrum of ethnic and religious holidays, many of which involve gifts. Between late October and early February, Christianity, Islam, Judaism, Hinduism, Wicca and other faiths all have major holidays that focus on family and tradition. Look for possibilities for gift tie-ins but also for books on food, decorating, and children's activities, as well as organizing and preserving memories.

Assignment 17: Finding "Hooks"

• Brainstorm ties between your book and seasons or holidays. Think about the business and back-to-school cycle, as well as winter, spring, summer and fall.

• Compile a list of local videographers and contact them to get rates. Be sure to check references and see examples of their work.

• Put together a list of companies that might want to use your book as a gift, reward or incentive. Then look for connections through your personal network.

"Been There, Done That" Author Tip:

"Don't launch your book into a vacuum! Beginning at least six months prior to your publication date, always develop and execute a comprehensive digital (online) promotional strategy to help get the word out about you and your book. This includes the following.

1) Find all the recent books that have been published (through self-publishing or traditional means) that are directly or indirectly competitive to yours. Track the online presence of these books and authors, and discover how and where they have been promoted (through blogs, online article databases, social media, publicity, internet radio, networking, organizations, strategic partnerships, etc.). Create your own digital grass-roots promotional strategy for your book, utilizing the best practices of successful competitive books.

2) Become an active participant in the national conversation about your book topic(s). Create your own blog, and post twice weekly. Research the existing blogs that cover the topic(s) of your book, and comment on these blogs regularly. (Be positive and empowering in your comments!) Supporting the online conversation about your topics builds your exposure and credibility. Always link back to your blog and your book site for readers to learn more about you and your work."

Kathy Caprino, M.A., author of *Breakdown, Breakthrough: The Professional Woman's Guide to Claiming a Life of Passion, Power, and Purpose.* www.breakdownbreakthrough.com and/or www.elliacommunications.com.

Chapter 18: *Launch Plus Five Months*

At this point, you probably have a couple of longer-term goals in mind. You may be looking to use the book to expand your speaking/consulting opportunities, or you may have an eye on writing another book. Now is the time to look for ways to leverage your visibility to create more opportunities or to promote your new book.

• If you have a publication date for a new book, begin planning for a "sneak peek" event.

• Pitch event organizers to consider you as a speaker for the next six month period. (In January, pitch for fall. In June, pitch for the next January.)

Sneak Peek Power

If you've cultivated a reader following (along with fans among bookstore managers and reviewers), you can use this built-in audience to your advantage when it comes time to launch your next book. Obviously, this is easier if your books are released within a year or so of each other than if they are farther apart. If you already know there is a follow-up book in the works, this is a good time to begin building anticipation.

Don't be shy about mentioning that you have another book coming up. Bookstore managers like to know you won't be a "one-hit wonder." Readers love it when an author that they enjoy has more to come. You can mention that you're working on the manuscript, and talk about your expected release date in your blog and on your website. As you progress and the details become more firm, you can hint more at the content and talk about your plans for the new book tour and promotion.

Once you've turned in the manuscript and done the edits, it's a great time to create a sneak peek. I do this every year on June 21, a date that is very significant in my Chronicles of the Necromancer fantasy series. I call it the "Hawthorn Moon Sneak Peek," named after a fictional holiday in my books. The sneak peek includes a special page on my site where I unveil the cover art for the new book and chapter excerpts. I also include interviews I've written with myself as well as interviews in the persona of my main characters, web audio of me reading from the upcoming book, and bonus downloads. It's been very popular, and has resulted in nice spikes in my web traffic and preorders. Of course, I also promote the online event with press releases to the major genre publications, links on my social media pages, and pre-event Twitter promotions. In addition, I invite a dozen or so bloggers and websites to be part of the event by hosting unique content.

You can create your own online sneak peek event for your next book. Always mention your upcoming book in your interviews and at live events. When you pitch event coordinators and the media, make sure you note that in addition to your current book, you are the author of a forthcoming book and give the title and release date/publisher. Remember to start all over again with the "Six Months Until Launch" tasks for the new book!

Look Ahead for Scheduling Events

Many events schedule their speakers at least six months in advance. Go back to the list of event planners you compiled prior to your launch. If you took notes as you made contact, you should see some upcoming event dates. This is a great time to re-contact these planners with a brand-new pitch. Now, you will have the added confidence that comes from having several months as a successful author under your belt.

If you've already spoken at an event, it's ok to ask to return. If you were a panelist before, perhaps you could be on a different panel, or handle a breakout, or even be a keynote speaker. Many events hold workshops and other mini-programs as options for attendees. Be creative and think of what you could provide before you contact the event planner. In my experience, most event planners are open to good ideas that add value and aren't just self-promotional. Make sure your topics are really targeted for the event's audience, and consider using a seasonal hook depending on when the event is scheduled.

Think out of the box. I've seen authors present craft or cooking demonstrations, give wine tastings and even take the audience on a bus tour. It depends on your area of expertise and your taste for adventure. For example, if you've written a book on local history (or ghost stories), offer to be the guide for a walking tour that highlights places of interest. If you're a food expert, create a limited sign-up extracurricular event that takes a dozen attendees on a dining tour of the best restaurants in the city. If your specialty is humor, offer to create a "humor break" mid-day to help people unwind. Or, if you're a yoga or exercise expert, see if the event planner would like to add an after-hours option that lets attendees stretch and relax. A budget expert could take a group to a grocery store to demonstrate thrifty shopping, or an organizer could do a hands-on seminar on clearing clutter. If you've written fiction and have great verbal storytelling skills, you might even offer to do a late-night "bedtime stories" session with a dramatized reading.

You don't have to be stuck behind a podium. Your speaking opportunities are limited only by your imagination. Event coordinators are always looking for something fresh and new, and audiences love a chance to participate by bringing resumes to critique, scenarios to problem-solve, and challenges in search of a solution.

Assignment 18: Long Term Goals
- Who could you tap for your push page? Think of the authors and providers of related services you've met, and look for web help on Elance.com.
- Compile your dream list of the events where you want to be asked to speak. Find out the dates, contacts and criteria and swing for the stars!

"Been There, Done That" Author Tip:
"Regardless of the type of tool you plan on using for your online promotions you should have a goal before you get started. Determining a goal in advance of creating the video can change the look of the video. For example, someone wanting to brand themselves in a more personal way might want to include a picture of themselves at the end of the video. Or you might put your name at the beginning and the end of the video for better name recognition and retention.

Where you place your video can also assist in fulfilling your pre-determined goal(s). Highlighting a genre or attracting attention of hobbyists can be done by placing your video on specialty sites or advertising to specific types of sites."

Sheila Clover English, CEO, COS (Circle of Seven) Productions
www.COSProductions.com

Chapter 19: *Launch Plus Six Months*

Now that you've been an author for six months, it's a good time for a little reflection. What marketing tasks have come naturally to you? What tasks were more of a struggle? We started out the marketing process by taking a skills inventory to get you going. Now that you have experience, how has that skills inventory changed? What new skills have you added? What processes can't you wait to be able to outsource?

This is also a good time to look at all the tools you've been using to see what will need to be revised for the coming months. Maybe you had a good idea for something different after your bookmarks were printed. Maybe you've seen another author with cool materials you can borrow and adapt. This is a good time to take stock and think about the changes you want to make.

In month six, it's time to:
- Update your website;
- Deepen your media ties; and
- Track your web success.

Revisiting the Web

Like most of us, you probably weren't quite sure how you were going to use your website when you created the first version before your launch. Maybe you've had the chance to make changes throughout this time, or perhaps you've been too busy to bother. Take a deep breath and look at your site with new eyes. Here are some ideas for ways to revise/expand your site.

• Build in better search engine optimization, keywords and metatagging to help your site rank better on searches.

• Refresh your photo, update your bio or add recent press releases, links to interviews and web audio/video to your site, or create a press page if you didn't have one before.

• Include reviewer comments.

- Revise/expand your online order page. Make sure you have an Amazon Affiliate link (You can find this on Amazon.com.), so that every time someone orders through your link you get extra cash!
- Link your blog, Twitter and other social networking sites to your website.
- Update pictures and video from your book tour.
- Expand on the content of your book with "free sample" related articles, tip sheets and quizzes.
- Add a user discussion board or comments page. Be careful to password protect this area or you will end up spending a lot of time removing spam.

You may want to revisit the goals for your website as you head into your second year as an author. If you intend to add speaking and spin-off products, perhaps your website needs an update to give these areas equal or additional space. Maybe you made the best of the free resources available to you at the time you prepared to launch, but could do better now with the luxury of a few months and a few more dollars. Or, perhaps you've spent some of your time this year looking at how other authors' websites work, and getting new ideas for your own site. This is a great time to get going on those ideas so your site will be ready for your next steps.

Take a Reporter to Lunch

While you're catching your breath between books, this is also a great time to get some feedback on your pitching technique. Email a few of the reporters, podcasters or radio hosts you seemed to hit it off best with, and ask them for their candid feedback on how you could do better. If they're local, it doesn't hurt to offer to talk over lunch or coffee, but don't be surprised if their schedules don't allow it. Most media folks will appreciate the thought. Take the advice to heart and improve your pitches. It would be even better if you take a course from a media coach to learn new tricks and hone your edge.

Get into the Numbers

If you haven't already started to use three free essential tools, now is the time. Google Keywords is a free keyword generator tool that will help you pick words for your content and headlines that get the most use in searches. The more frequently-used a word is, the more times content using that word will be indexed by search engines. When that word is relevant to your book and you use that word frequently in your content, your site is more likely to turn up high in the search engine results.

Use Google Keywords to check the popularity of the phrases you use frequently and see if there are more powerful substitutes, and then update your content. You can also use this program to suggest additional tags or keywords to use in your blogging and "#words" to help elevate your Twitter Tweets.

Google Analytics is another free program that helps you understand your web traffic. Now that your book has been out for a while, take a look at where your web traffic comes from. How many hits come from referring sites? How many come from direct links (people typing in your website address)? How many come from search engines?

Now look at the top referring sites. This can give you a good idea of which sites you want to continue to partner with or to post information on. Google Analytics also shows you which pages of your site get the most traffic. You'll also find out how many first-time visitors you've gotten, how much overall traffic you've received, and how long the average visitor stays on your website.

This last information is referred to as "stickiness." Having a *sticky* site is considered to be better than a non-sticky site. The longer someone stays on your site, the more interested they're assumed to be in your topic/ book and the more useful information they are discovering. In contrast, your "bounce rate" is the percentage of people who never go deeper than your first page. If you find that your bounce rate is very high, and your stickiness very low, you may want to consult a web designer to help you make the site more user-friendly.

Google Alerts uses the keywords you give it to send you an email every time those keywords show up on Google. Obviously you don't want to use broad, generic keywords for your topic or you'll fill up your inbox with irrelevant alerts. However, you should set Google Alerts at a minimum for your name, your book title, the top keywords related to your title, maybe even the names of authors whose work is similar to yours. This way you'll know whenever anyone posts a review or comment about you or your book, or when someone picks up one of your press releases or articles. It's also an easy way to follow what another author is doing if there's someone you'd like to learn from by example.

If you set your Google Alert keywords early in the promotion process, you may want to revise those words to make them fit your needs more tightly. You may have also discovered some great new keywords to add. Remember, every time you get a Google Alert about a review, article, interview or press release that posts, you can put that link in your online press room and submit it to Digg.com and other social bookmarking sites to make it easy for others to find it.

Assignment 19: Keep Your Website Fresh
- Look over your website to see how to apply the changes discussed in this chapter.
- Take the time to build and extend your relationship with key media people.
- Update your settings on Google Alerts and Google Analytics, and make the most of Google Keywords.

"Been There, Done That" Author Tip:
"One of the easiest, cheapest and most well-received things I tried was the book trailer. You don't need expensive equipment. We did it with our digital camera and a memory card. Since my book was about a magic-wielding pirate, we chose Pirate's Day at the Carolina Renaissance Festival, and encouraged people in costume to say "Arrr!" for the camera. My husband edited the footage with a free program he found online, I created text pages to intersperse, and before we knew it, we had a book trailer! My publisher liked it enough to put it on the website, and I've received emails from people who had it forwarded to them. There's nothing like a little viral marketing to get the word out."

Misty Massey, author of *Mad Kestral* www.MistyMassey.com

Chapter 20: *Now What?*

Congratulations on surviving an exciting and challenging year. Now, you're not only a published author, you're becoming a seasoned promoter for your book and your own platform.

As you move into Year 2, there is still a lot of unexplored territory. Although you may feel as if you never stopped moving, and that you've visited every bookstore in the world, the truth is that you've probably overlooked or bypassed some conferences, book clubs and bookstores that are worth scheduling for the coming year.

Think about all the other authors you've met, those who are also just beginning their careers, and those who have been publishing for decades. You can learn a lot from listening and asking questions. These are the perfect mentors, not only about marketing your book, but about agents, editors, and publishing in general. Listen also to readers for clues on what types of books they seek out, what other venues they frequent, and how they consume information.

The issue of *consuming information* is particularly important because readers are finding that they enjoy their books in a variety of formats. Mass-market paperbacks, trade paperbacks, graphic novels, e-books, audiobooks, and even serialized podcast dramas are all formats to consider and explore. Books also are "reincarnated" into workshops, teleclasses, home-study courses, coaching cards, DVDs, and branded products. Your book may or may not make it to the big screen via Hollywood, but there is plenty of opportunity to promote and sell your work via web video, DVDs, and for non-fiction authors, training and educational video.

Each step you take in providing content through different venues broadens your personal and professional platform. You grow from being an author to becoming a speaker, then a thought leader and a national expert. Along the way, new opportunities open as do additional career choices. Those opportunities come because you have made yourself visible as an expert, not just because you wrote a book. Marketing yourself is the key.

You may also be planning one or more additional books. These books may be part of a series or may go in another direction entirely. Thanks to what you've learned this year—both in terms of what worked for you and what didn't—you can leverage that knowledge into greater success for your new books.

Writing is a passion. Publishing, however, is a business. The bold truth is that to be able to afford to continue your passion, it helps to be commercially successful as a business. Marketing brings passion and profit together by enabling the largest number of people to experience and benefit from the information you have written. Good luck and may you soar as high as your dreams will take you.

Planning Calendar and Launch Promotional

Checklist

Launch in 6 Months
- ꙮ Create your business plan and your marketing plan.
- ꙮ Create your time and money budget.
- ꙮ Compile a media list and a list of potential reviewers.
- ꙮ Determine your time availability and set up a master calendar.
- ꙮ Based on your time and travel budget, determine the geographic area in which you can make live appearances.
- ꙮ Research the bookstores and events appropriate to your topic and business goals within that geographic area.
- ꙮ Compile a list of bookstore managers and event coordinators.
- ꙮ Set up a website and/or blog.
- ꙮ Set up a Facebook page and a Twitter profile.
- ꙮ Investigate other social media sites where your target audience of readers is already congregating.

Launch in 5 Months
- ꙮ Write your pitch for bookstores and events.
- ꙮ Research options for printing bookmarks, posters, business cards, etc. (Don't forget to factor these into your budget.)
- ꙮ Find out from your publisher (or directly from your artist if you are self-published) any limitations you might have in using your book cover art for promotional purposes.
- ꙮ Compile your speaker/author bio.

Launch in 4 Months
- ꙮ Write your media pitch, reviewer letter and press kit.
- ꙮ Set up speaking engagements or book signings.

Launch in 3 Months
- ꙮ Add content to your website.
- ꙮ Blog regularly about your topic.
- ꙮ Use social media to stir up excitement.
- ꙮ Send out your review copies.

Launch in 2 Months
- Create your "push page."
- Start uploading to article directories.
- Write your press releases.

Launch in 1 Month
- Create your media blitz.
- Recruit your street team.
- Post your tour schedule and finalize contest details.

Launch!
- Make the most of your signings and events.
- Remain visible with social media and PR.

Launch Plus 1 Month
- Build connections with other authors.
- Use social media to keep buzz going.
- Catch-up on important tasks.

Launch Plus 2 Months
- Explore getting a virtual assistant.
- Update or add easy tech additions like Google Analytics, Google Keyword Tool, Google Alerts, etc.

Launch Plus 3 Months
- Look for ways to expand your platform, such by creating your own teleseminars, workshops and live events or co-creating programs and promotions with other authors or thought leaders.
- Have your book reformatted as an e-book.
- Discover non-bookstore opportunities.

Launch Plus 4 Months
- Make the most of reviews.
- Prepare for new live events.
- Explore seasonal or gift "hooks" for your book.

Launch Plus 5 Months

- Begin planning for a "sneak peek" event for your next book.
- Pitch event organizers to consider you as a speaker for the next six-month period.

Launch Plus 6 Months

- Take a skills inventory.
- Update your website.
- Deepen your media ties.
- Track your web success.

About the Author

Gail Z. Martin is an author, entrepreneur and educator. She owns DreamSpinner Communications and is your "Get Results" resource for marketing strategies that work. Gail specializes in helping coaches, consultants, authors, small businesses and solo professionals get marketing results. Her teleseminars share powerful marketing techniques and her nonfiction articles have been featured in over forty regional and national magazines. She is also the host of the *Shared Dreams* Podcast about marketing (SharedDreamsPodcast.com) and the host of *Ghost in the Machine* (GhostInTheMachinePodcast.com.) You can find her online at DreamSpinnerCommunications.com, GailMartinMarketing.com, on Facebook and on Twitter.com/GailMartinPR.

Gail is the creator of the Solopreneur Survival Guide home study course and resource kits. She is also the author of two e-books, *154 Power-Packed PR and Marketing Tips* and *Profit, Passion* and *Partnership: Entrepreneur Success Strategies.* Gail is a frequent speaker for organizations that include Microsoft Partner Edge Network, Pitchrate, MarketingProfs, PR Newswire, eWomenNetwork, WriteWellU.com, 911MarketingHelp.com, SmartWomensCafe.com and the University of North Carolina—Charlotte. She presents lively programs on social media, PR and marketing for audiences across North America and to international audiences via webcasts and teleseminars.

In addition to her marketing career, Gail is the author of the bestselling Chronicles of the Necromancer fantasy adventure series, which includes: *The Summoner; The Blood King; Dark Haven;* and *Dark Lady's Chosen.* Her fiction site is www.ChroniclesOfTheNecromancer.com, she's on Twitter.com/GailZMartin and you can also find her on MySpace.

For new updates and more book marketing tips, tricks and secrets, visit www.ThriftyAuthor.com and follow Gail at www.Twitter.com/GailMartinPR

LaVergne, TN USA
20 July 2010
190182LV00002B/5/P